In Search of the Holy Grail and the Precious Blood

Edinburgh

Dublin

Liverpool

Esbjerg   Copenhagen

Glastonbury London   Harwich   Hamburg   Hanover

Penzance   Bruges   Magdeburg

Plymouth Portsmouth   Aachen

                          Brussels

                  Fécamp

              Caen   Reims   Nuremberg   Prague

Brocéliande   Paris   Vienna

              Troyes   Strasbourg

         Bourges   Basel   Innsbruck

      Charroux   Ljubljana

                                St. Maurice

Lugo   Santander   Domme   Genoa

                  Toulouse

Zaragoza   Foix

Madrid   Sant Pere   Rome

              de Rodes

              Barcelona

                  Valencia   Naples   Otranto

Jaén

In Search of the Holy Grail and the Precious Blood

A Travellers' Guide

Deike and Ean Begg

iUniverse, Inc.
New York   Bloomington   Shanghai

In Search of the Holy Grail and the Precious Blood
A Travellers' Guide

iUniverse books may be ordered through booksellers or by contacting:

iUniverse
1663 Liberty Drive
Bloomington, IN 47403
www.iuniverse.com
1-800-Authors (1-800-288-4677)

Because of the dynamic nature of the Internet, any Web addresses or links contained in this book may have changed since publication and may no longer be valid.

The views expressed in this work are solely those of the author and do not necessarily reflect the views of the publisher, and the publisher hereby disclaims any responsibility for them.

ISBN: 978-0-595-49872-7 (pbk)
ISBN: 978-0-595-61286-4 (ebk)

Printed in the United States of America

… the mysterious something that inspired the knightly orders (the Templars, for instance), and that seems to have found expression in the Grail legend, may possibly have been the germ of a new orientation in life, in other words, a nascent symbol.

C. G. JUNG (COLLECTED WORKS 6, PAR. 409)

Table of Contents

Acknowledgements

Our thanks are due first of all to the authors, named and anonymous, of the scores of local guides without whose labours we could not have written this book. They are too numerous and their books too difficult to obtain, except on the spot, to be included in what is a very select Bibliography.

There are many others who helped us in various ways to whom we also owe a debt of gratitude. They know what they did and will, we hope, excuse us for not going into detail.

PHOTOGRAPHS

All photographs are by the authors except for the Grail-Stone at Jaén by Jennifer Begg.

MAPS

Great Britain—Ordinance Survey 1986 Motoring Atlas of Great Britain.

Rest of Europe—Michelin. The larger and smaller Michelin maps use somewhat different formats which accounts for apparent discrepancies in the map references.

Foreword

Our modern world seems to have lost that fascination and compulsion which once drew so many into pilgrimage. No longer are we enticed by an inner urge to uproot our lives and, with scant regard for the difficulties, to head for distant sacred sites. The whole concept of pilgrimage now appears anachronistic, irrelevant to the host of other demands that we face. To take time out, to pursue a measured and deliberate journey, devoid of all electronic sustenance and stimulation, seems a wildly eccentric enterprise. And yet, when we are stilled for a moment, when we allow ourselves a respite from television's bland soundbites and our computer's flickering pixels, the question arises: where indeed are we going? And why?

'Know thyself', wisely commanded the ancient guardians of the mysteries. They understood well that to know oneself was the beginning of wisdom. But how is such a task commenced?

It begins with a journey. The pursuit of Self-knowledge is a pilgrimage. And in this pilgrimage the outer journey reflects the inner journey; it serves to focus that inner process through a series of stages until the outer coincides with the inner and the pilgrim truly knows him or herself. This finds expression in the medieval Grail quest, itself a pilgrimage: in the *Perlesvaus,* when a knight finally confronts the Grail within its associated vision of Light, the question is posed, 'Whom does the Grail serve?' It serves, of course, that inner Divine spark.

Deike and Ean Begg have revitalized the idea of pilgrimage. As they have earlier written, it has all but vanished in the Protestant Christian world. Yet, they explain, the embers of the Pilgrim instinct lie deep within us all and cry out to be fanned into a real and renovating fire. For almost all other religions this instinct remains a vital part of the living faith. We are all aware of the importance of pilgrimages to Mecca, Jerusalem and Rome to name but those centres of faiths which share a common origin in the monotheism of Abraham

This book, *In Search of the Holy Grail and the Precious Blood,* is an impressively researched compilation of those historical facts which concern the large number of holy sites in Europe devoted to the Grail and the Precious Blood. Together with these accounts is woven a rich collection of baroque and mysterious legends which have grown up around these ancient places of pilgrimage. It is a difficult task for any writer to move with equal facility between fact and legend without degrading the value of either but the authors have created a sensitive perspective within which such moves are natural, indeed vital, to our deeper understanding. There is not another book like it.

Legend has a value quite different from that of history. What is important for a pilgrim is not a record of exactly what occurred but rather the meaning of that ancient event. Legend has an eternal quality which transcends the arid recitation of fact. The pilgrim has a need not of history but of eternity, however many hesitant steps that might take to understand.

A pilgrim is not seeking to discover something new but is seeking to remember that which the Soul has always known. And in this search it helps to stand amidst the sacred groves and stones in order that this archaic memory might be triggered. The authors have given all of us a host of sacred sites where, on our Journey, any of us might, for an instant, remember.

MICHAEL BAIGENT

Introduction

The Holy Grail: what magic the name conjures up even for those who have forgotten its story. It is the ultimate quest and the one that most characterises the adventurous spirit of the West. It has become a metaphor for all that is most desirable and hardest to achieve.

Mysteries are by definition hidden and secret. But is there any light that can be thrown on the supreme mystery that is the Grail? If it was the Cup of the Last Supper then it is the symbol of divine love that, stemming from the Sacred Heart of the Cosmic Christ, gently penetrates the souls of all who obey the new commandment of Maundy Thursday: 'Love one another'. If it is the Celtic cauldron of rebirth and inexhaustible nourishment it offers each of us the strength and courage to pass through the day and the world in the memory of our true selves and our purpose here on earth. The Grail King who lies in our interior castle, guarding the vessel which contains the secret of our real identity, is, perhaps, none other than our own inner god who sent us forth on our quest of soul-making.

The many versions of the Grail legend are too diverse to summarise, but the main elements are these:

1. Something has gone wrong. The world has run out of meaning and it is women who first sense this. The old king, standing for the established order, is impotent and the land is waste.

2. A youthful hero, typically an orphan, is destined to find the Grail, heal the old king and take his place. Two or three other chosen ones may share his vision and his quest. The Grail is glimpsed and then lost because a vital question has not been asked. This may be a failure of compassion in which the hero neglects to ask the old king what he is suffering; or it may be a failure of understanding what the Grail is for and whom it serves.

3. The Grail itself is active: something is operating in human lives that transcends conscious intentions. It names those who are to be its servants and

leads them on their individual quest. It designates the high places where its presence will be commemorated and is the architect of the Grail castles and temples.

4. There is a fellowship or family of the Grail who continue to further and protect its interests in the world.

The Grail itself assumes many forms, but in all of them it radiates a supernaturally brilliant light. In the first version, that of Chrétien de Troyes (c. 1180), it is a magical dish, carried by a maiden, which serves each guest with the food he most desires. Later it became associated with the Cup of the Last Supper. It has also been seen as a cauldron, a stone, a book, a human head, a table, or an ark (in both senses). Among modern writers, Baigent, Leigh and Lincoln present a fascinating case for the Grail being itself the Holy Blood that still flows in the veins of families descended from the union of Jesus and Mary Magdalen and the line of David.

At the Crucifixion, Longinus, the blind centurion (see **Mantua**), pierced the side of Christ, causing the precious blood to flow. Joseph of Arimathea caught this in the cup used by Jesus and his disciples at the Last Supper. Joseph was imprisoned for forty years, during which time he received secret teaching from Jesus and was nourished by the Grail. According to legend, Joseph, after his release, crossed the seas with a few followers, including Bron(s), the Rich Fisher, to Marazion in Cornwall. He eventually settled in **Glastonbury**, where he founded the first church in Britain. One night, centuries later, the Grail brought by Joseph appeared to King Arthur and his knights as they were gathered at the Round Table. Borne by two angels it hovered above them in all its splendour and mystery filling all who beheld it with a sense of holy awe. The Grail then vanished, and Merlin, Arthur's spiritual guide, inspired the knights to set out one by one in quest of it.

The mysterious force of the Grail drew them, like the *eternal feminine* in Goethe's *Faust*, 'onward and upward', beyond their existing boundaries and known capabilities, urging them to try this way or that, to risk failure and make fools of themselves, until the chosen few came to experience the ultimate Grail reality: union with the divine. For eight centuries, after its appearance in the pages of Chrétien de Troyes, the mysterious, indefinable symbol that is the Grail has continued to point seekers towards the purpose and meaning of individual existence.

New symbols emerge when the times demand them. What was it about the twelfth century that needed the Grail? As Christendom emerged from the Dark Ages, its great unifying goal was the deliverance of Jerusalem and the Holy Places from Islam. In 1099 the First Crusade under Godefroy de Bouillon (allegedly descended from Jesus and Mary Magdalen) freed Jerusalem, and a Kingdom was established there to ratify the victory of the Cross in the city of David.

Once again, pilgrims were able to flock to the Holy Land and reassure themselves about the historical and geographical facts of their faith. But the triumph, won through massacres and injustice, foundered over the next century amid internecine quarrels, incompetence and the dazzling victories of a new Saracen leader, Saladin. With access denied to the sacred centre of the world, pilgrimage became increasingly an inner quest. At this very moment of crisis and defeat, the Grail emerged as a beacon of hope and consolation into the consciousness of the West. But the Grail, for all its glory as the dominant motif of European literature, was never fully assimilated or accepted by the Catholic Church. The movement associated with it had its roots in places other than Rome.

It grew out of what was called the *matière de Bretagne,* the legends and myths of the Celtic peoples preserved by bards and disseminated in translation through the courts of France and England. The Grail appeared at that point in the Arthurian story when victory had been achieved by the fellowship of the Round Table. Now, a new idea was needed to stir the knights out of their complacent round of feasting and tournaments. In the various accounts it is women who tell the men that something is wrong: the old order is stagnant and a new vision is needed. The Table gradually emptied, the fellowship broke up and each knight set out on his solitary search. It is no coincidence that the luxurious courts, established by the victorious crusaders in the Near East, had certain similarities to Camelot in its period of decadence.

It was, however, not just Jerusalem that was lost. An alternative Church, that of Love, Amor, the inversion of Roma, was murderously suppressed by Christian crusaders. It was a religion centred on the Languedoc, based on St John's Gospel of love, that honoured women as teachers and priestesses and rejected the formal sacraments of Catholicism. This was Catharism, part of the old Gnostic stream, whose source was Alexandria and which came to the West directly through the cult of Mary Magdalen and her companions, in the fifth century. It also permeated Europe indirectly via Armenia, Byzantium, Bulgaria, the Bosnian Bogomils and the heretics of Lombardy. Its tentacles were everywhere, reaching as far as the Rhineland, Flanders, Champagne and England. But its headquarters was the Languedoc, where it was firmly established by 1180. Here the Albigensian Crusade was launched in 1209 to extirpate it. Its last stronghold, **Montségur**, fell in 1244.

The connection between the Cathars and the Grail has been much debated. What is certain is that these two streams, Catharism and Grail Christianity, in which the heresies of the East fused with the Druidic-Celtic Church of the West, coexisted as expressions of the spirit of the age that did not see eye to eye with Rome.

They met in the *Parzival* of Wolfram von Eschenbach, the towering genius of the Grail tradition. It was not through conventional Catholicism and its sacraments that the hero achieved the Grail, but through the teaching of wise hermits, similar to Merlin and the Cathar Parfaits.

The troubadours, the poet-minstrels of Languedoc, propagated, in a hidden way, the teachings of Catharism through innumerable hymns of praise to love and La Dame, not quite the same as the official Our Lady to whom the Church was erecting great cathedrals throughout Europe. The troubadours' Lady was sometimes representative of Catharism itself, but sometimes also seen, with astonishing psychological insight, as that inner feminine other that is the object of man's quest and love and needs to be experienced with a real woman. This was their expression of the Grail quest. The troubadours were condemned eventually, along with Catharism. The urge to honour the feminine became restricted to the official cult of the Virgin Mary and Catholic marriage. Arid male intellectual scholasticism ruled the universities. To the Inquisition's repression of heretics was added the persecution of witches. Women lost all the rights and privileges that they had enjoyed, both in Celtdom and Catharism. Even the practice of their traditional skills, especially healing, was criminalised and punished by torture and death.

It seemed, by the beginning of the fourteenth century, that the light of the Holy Grail had failed. The great lords and ladies of the Grail, such as Eleanor of Aquitaine, Richard Coeur de Lion and Frederick II of Hohenstaufen, belonged to a past that had refused to be bounded by rules and labels, whether sexual or religious. Eleanor left the king of France to marry the king of England. She inspired courtly love and the Courts of Love, through which people felt their way towards a new male-female relationship. Frederick took all knowledge as his domain, filling his court at Palermo with Jewish and Muslim scholars as well as great astrologer-mages like Michael Scot. Instead of leading a Crusade against Jerusalem he simply did a deal with the Saracens. Both he and the Lionheart, Eleanor's favourite son, were thoroughly unpopular with the papacy for their individualistic and unorthodox beliefs and behaviour.

The last Cathars were not rounded up until several decades into the fourteenth century, by which time another great calamity had befallen the forces of enlightenment. The Knights Templars, whom Wolfram named as the Guardians of the Grail, were driven from their power-base in Outremer (the Near East) with the fall of the Latin Kingdom of Jerusalem, and returned to the West, especially France. Their great wealth and influence aroused the envy of Philip the Fair, King of France. At dawn, on Friday 13 October 1307, he struck, arresting all members of the Order in his domains. Accused of heresy, blasphemy and sexual vice, they were tortured and killed. Philip's creature, Pope Clement, dissolved the Order in 1312. Not all Templars perished, but continued to flourish under other names in other lands, like Scotland, Portugal, Spain and Germany. In England it was claimed that the Templars had become infected with the alleged abominations of Catharism. Earlier, they had declined to take part in the Albigensian Crusade and even protected the persecuted Cathars. This same terrible fourteenth century also witnessed the outbreak of the Black Death and the Hundred Years War, two of the greatest scourges ever to afflict Europe.

What became of the Grail movement? Its servants went underground and survived as alchemists, Freemasons, Rosicrucians, artists and astrologers. The tarot deck emerged as the living testament to the Cathar/Grail doctrine of transformation. Another testimony is to be found in the series of tapestries in the Cluny Museum in Paris, known as *The Lady of the Unicorn,* in which the unicorn, persecuted and penned in, stands for the remnants of Catharism.

Official Christianity was infiltrated by the Grail movement in a way that could be accepted by the conventionally devout and was free of any apparent trace of heresy. It was Robert de Boron, in *c.* 1200, who first identified the Grail with the Cup of the Last Supper. This is the vessel now venerated in **Valencia** Cathedral, whose earlier history had strong links to the Grail movement in Aragon (see San Juan de la Peña). At Genoa, a rival Grail, the *Sacro Catino,* was also accorded the highest honours. Traditions of ancient Celtic cauldrons of healing and rebirth were brought under the aegis of the Church and occasionally performed similar miraculous functions. Many other jars and vases from antiquity, some considered to be the one in which Jesus turned water into wine, became sacred relics and goals of pilgrimage. Black Madonnas, harking back to pagan goddesses and, perhaps, secret traditions concerning Mary Magdalen as the Grail-bearer, were enthroned in the most popular shrines of Europe. Saints whom the official Church viewed with some suspicion, like Joseph of Arimathea, Nicodemus, Lazarus, Longinus and Amadour, were inextricably intertwined with Grail Christianity and could not be wholly excluded from the calendar, especially when miracles confirmed their prestige and popularity. The Cistercians, whose greatest leader, St Bernard, wrote the rule of the Order of the Temple, made a great effort to incorporate the Grail within Catholicism in the first half of the thirteenth century, but it never quite caught on with Rome.

So, apart from **Langport** in Somerset, where a medieval stained-glass window shows Joseph of Arimathea with the two cruets containing the blood and

xviii   In Search of the Holy Grail and the Precious Blood

sweat of Christ, the mysterious **Rosslyn Chapel** in Scotland and the modern Grail Church of **Tréhorenteuc** in **Brocéliande**, Brittany, you will seldom see the Grail depicted in churches.

The impetus of the Grail movement within the Church was transformed into the Cult of the Sacred Heart of Jesus and the Immaculate Heart of Mary, in which its symbolic meaning was worthily preserved and amplified. Before that, the focus had been on the related cult of the Precious Blood.

There are four major sources for relics of the Precious Blood:

1 Blood collected at or after the Crucifixion by Joseph of Arimathea, Nicodemus, Mary Magdalen or Longinus.

2 Blood from a 'miracle', such as that which took place in Beirut in 765, when an image of Christ was crucified and pierced by Jews, releasing large enough quantities of the precious liquid to satisfy the growing demand for such relics in the West. No doubt **Heilgenblut** is a distorted memory of this event.

3 Miracles in which the blood and wine of the Eucharist turned spontaneously into the literal body and blood of Christ (see **Bois-Seigneur-Isaac**, **Bolsena**, **O Cebreiro** et al).

4 Particles of blood of unknown provenance, like that found in the supposed tomb of St Philomena. There are a few miracles of liquefying blood belonging to various saints, the most famous being St Januarius of Naples. We have included St Pantaleon because we continually found traces of him and his hermetic background along the way (see **Ravello** and **San Pantaleón** et al).

We should add here an appendage to the cult, stemming from the only known shedding of the divine blood prior to the Passion: that which flowed from the Circumcision of Jesus. This tradition led us on a merry dance in search of the Holy Foreskin (see **Calcata**, **Charroux** and **Niedermünster**).

It may seem surprising that such apparently literal avidity for relics could be connected with the subtleties of Grail Christianity. The connection is to be found first of all in the sites, many of which were holy long before the advent of Christianity and are places of power belonging to the sacred geography of Europe. Then there are the many saints who have re-potentised these shrines with their presence and prayers. Finally, the miracles—especially of healing—

so well attested for so long at many of these sites, convinced us that literal pilgrimages to them bring their own blessings.

Apart from the Holy Grail and the Holy Blood, we have included sites associated with the Holy Lance. The Church has grown now wary of this cult (see **St Maurice, Vienna** and **Nuremberg**) and seeks to dissociate itself from it to the extent that the Vatican museum now denies any knowledge of the spear-relic it once possessed.

In fact the lance had a healthy Judaeo-Christian background, being made by Phineas, grandson of Aaron, according to a legend, admittedly transmitted by the Gnostic, Ephrem the Syrian. Saul, in his madness, hurled it at David, and it was later used by Longinus to pierce the side of Christ and release blood and water into the Grail. But it became suspect to the Church as the spear of Lug, the Celtic sun-god who possessed all skills and, above all, as Gungnir, the spear of death and victory, belonging to Wotan, the most repressed of all the pre-Christian gods. That Hitler took an interest in it did nothing to increase its respectability. It now resides in the Hofburg in Vienna. What was strongly believed to be the Spear of Longinus surfaced at Antioch thanks to a vision granted to a monk called Bartholomew in 1098 during the First Crusade. It passed for a time into the hands of the Count of Toulouse. This was presumably the relic discovered by Saint Helena, mother of the Emperor Constantine, along with the True Cross and other instruments of the Passion. The Lance was for a time in the possession of the Emperor of the East in Constantinople, who pawned the head, later redeemed it and sent it to Saint Louis IX of France. The rest of the Lance remained in Constantinople until the fall of the city in 1453, when it passed to Sultan Mohammed II. His son, Bajazet, gave it to the Grand Master of the Knights of Saint John of Jerusalem in exchange for certain favours. The Grand Master, in turn, gave it to the Pope. It was received with rejoicing in Rome in 1492 and placed in Saint Peter's.

At the end of the eighteenth century, the Grail movement resurfaced with English and German Romanticism. It flowered in the second half of the nineteenth century in the poetry of Tennyson and, above all, in the alliance of King Ludwig II of Bavaria and Richard Wagner, to reawaken the spirit of Wolfram von Eschenbach and the *Minnesänger*. Their aim was to form a new art that embraced poetry, opera and architecture (see **The Grail Castles of Germany**).

After the two world wars of the twentieth century it seems that the old order and the old certainties are passing away. Communism, capitalism and Christianity are all under question. In Britain few have much faith in the impregnable establishments of yesteryear. Even the monarchy no longer seems unassailable. Long ago two women, Guinevere and Morgan-le-Fay, engineered the fall of Arthur's House of Pendragon. Could much the same be happening today to the House of Windsor?

What of the future? Two of the great prophets of the New Age of Aquarius (whose symbol has always been the Cup) were deeply concerned with the meaning of the Grail. One was Rudolf Steiner who built a modern Grail Castle at **Dornach** and inspired many writings on the history and meaning of the Grail. The other was Carl Gustav Jung. He left to his wife Emma and his closest collaborator Marie-Louise von Franz the honour of investigating the subject, which culminated in their important book, *The Grail Legend.* He himself lived much of the myth in his own life. When he was lost in the wasteland and the perilous forest during the First World War, after he renounced his role as Freud's heir apparent and set out to find his own way, it was a woman, Toni Wolff, who helped him on his journey. At the end of this experience he had a vision of the dead returning from Jerusalem, angry, because they had not found what they were seeking in conventional religion. Later, he had a dream that he was to swim to an island off the coast of Britain and bring back the Grail. For many this is precisely what he has done—regenerated the quest for the truth within, for those disillusioned by Round Tables and establishments, politics, technology and churches.

The quest is clearly an inner one. So why did we pursue it so literally, zig-zagging wildly across Europe in search of spear-heads, phials of blood, large pots and little prepuces? We are both depth psychotherapists who walk happily amidst a forest of symbols, for whom literalisation is anathema. Our book, *On the Trail of Merlin,* had brought us, as it were, as far as the Round Table, so the next project that Merlin proposed, the Holy Grail, seemed a logical sequel for us. But more than logic was involved. So much of our work is in the wasteland of male-female relationships, where the old paths and guidelines have disappeared, that we wanted to make this project *our* Holy Grail. It was a mad idea that only Parzival, the Pure Fool, could understand. Our one-month honeymoon was spent each night but two in a different place, driving 4,000 miles through twelve countries, doing our research as we went along. We started by arriving at the ferry with a ticket a month out of date. Later we broke down on the Vienna-Graz motorway in a heat-wave, having filled our diesel-tank with petrol. The next day we embarked on the unknown perils of former Yugoslavia without car insurance. There were some nights when we found no room at the inn.

However crazy the experience, we recommend it to all like-minded fools. For what is inner calls for incarnation on the outside and any outer pilgrimage is but a symbolic enactment of the inward quest—to where? Perhaps Cana of

Galilee, where Jesus turned water into wine at the wedding of an unknown couple, believed by some to have been his two beloved disciples, John the Divine
and Mary Magdalen. From this mystical inner marriage flowed two of the
major sources of Grail Christianity: the Cathar Gospel of Love and the ideal of
feminine wisdom. For us, a lapsed Lutheran and a heretical Gnostic Catholic, it
was apparently sheer chance that brought us to examine the possible meaning
of interior marriage in Reichenau, on August 15, Feast of the Assumption. This
is the day when the feminine principle annually celebrates the restoration of its
divine rights. Here we received the Body and Blood of Christ for the first time.
We also discovered in that very church what was claimed to be the vessel, called
the Kana-Krug, in which Christ performed his first miracle, which proclaimed,
to those that had ears to hear, the meaning of his mission.

The British Isles

The British Isles map showing: Iona, Scone, Rosslyn Chapel, Edinburgh/Arthur's Seat, Lough Erne, Richmond, Peel/Isle of Man, Dublin, Dinas Bran, Bardsey Island, Hailes Abbey, Ashridge, Caerleon-upon-Usk, London, Glastonbury, Taunton, South Cadbury, Winchester, Penzance

England and Wales

*

—Ashridge—

Map 24, SP 9912
5km north of Berkhamsted

The origins of the cult of the Holy Blood at the monastery of **Ashridge** are similar to those of **Hailes Abbey** (qv) in that both were granted their sacred relics by Edmund, the last Earl of Cornwall, who actually founded Ashridge in 1283 and died there in 1300.

Douglas Coult, the author of *A Prophet of Ashridge,* to whom we are indebted for most of our information concerning this site, records the tradition that it was in Mantua, the main source of the Holy Blood in Europe, that Edmund was granted a portion in recognition of some service he had rendered the city. More plausibly he purchased the relic from the Count of Flanders (see **Bruges** and **Weingarten**).

Hailes was a Cistercian Abbey, but the order associated with Ashridge is highly mysterious and unique in England. They were called Bonhommes (good men), a title that was suspect enough to be taboo in orthodox circles as that adopted by heretical Cathar Perfecti (see **Montségur** et passim). Certainly Edmund's family on his mother's side, the Counts of Toulouse, were, notoriously, protectors of the Cathars. Although the open warfare of the Albigensian Crusade came to an end with the fall of **Montségur** in 1244, the persecution of suspected Cathars continued for another century and influential sympathisers no doubt continued to provide refuge for them wherever possible.

One such sympathiser may have been the Black Prince, son of Edward III, who made him the first Duke of Cornwall in 1337. He was the greatest scourge of the kings of France, the main beneficiaries of the Albigensian Crusade. He captured the French King John at the Battle of Poitiers (1356) and brought him

1

back to the Tower of London where he languished for twenty-five years. The Black Prince was also the Prince of Aquitaine which included many of the old Cathar strongholds. He was the second founder of the college of Bonhommes at Ashridge and bequeathed to it 'our great table of gold and silver, furnished full of precious relics, and in the middle of it a holy cross of the wood of the True Cross, and the said table is garnished with stones and pearls, that is to say twenty-five rubies, thirty-four sapphires, fifteen great pearls and several other sapphires, emeralds and small pearls …'

If, as has been suggested, the Holy Grail was sent by the Templars of Aragon to England after the fall of **Montségur** it is not improbable that Edmund of Cornwall would have become its custodian. Ashridge, built in the midst of a forest as a house of pleasure and hunting-lodge, served by Bonhommes, would have furnished an appropriate safe haven.

An eighteenth-century visitor to Ashridge, the historian Newcome, saw the wall paintings still extant on the old cloisters as evidence for the Cathar connection, since they satirised the Dominicans and Franciscans, who were charged with repressing the heresy through the Inquisition. Wall paintings, discovered in 1953 at 68 Piccotts End, Hemel Hempstead, a hostel for pilgrims to Ashridge, have been considered to uphold this view.

The monastery and its ancient crypt are closed to the public, but the gardens are open Monday to Thursday 2-5pm; Saturday, Sunday, Bank Holiday Monday 2-5.30pm.

—Bardsey Island—

Map 44, SH 1221

Here Merlin took the thirteen hallows of Britain which included the Cauldron of Dyrnwch, the Drinking Horn of Bran and the Sword of Rhydderch Hael. Taliesin, the reincarnating sixth-century bard, often identified with Merlin and named by Tennyson as a Knight of the Round Table, drank from the crystal cup (see *On the Trail of Merlin*).

—Caerleon-upon-Usk—

Map 20, ST 3391

This was the seat of Arthur's Court from which the Quest for the Holy Grail originated.

—Dinas Bran/Llangollen—

Map 46, Sf2142, marked Castell

Dinas Bran is the most likely site of the Grail castle in Britain. In medieval literature it was known as Corbenic, a derivation of the name raven or crow. Bran, whose name also means raven, possessed a life-restoring cauldron, one of the prototypes of the Holy Grail. He is often associated with Bron, the Fisher King, son-in-law of Joseph of Arimathea (who brought the Grail to Britain) and grandfather of Perceval. Bran was also wounded in the leg and his life bears many other resemblances to that of the Fisher King. Bran's head, which provided nourishment like a Grail, was eventually buried at the Tower of London until exhumed by Arthur. His ravens there continue to guard the land. In a medieval romance, Fulk Fitzwarren comes, like Perceyal/Peredur, to the Chastel Merveil—also known as Chastel Bran—in the Welsh Marches, meets the Fisher King and is invited as an honoured guest to the castle.

The situation of the castle is outstanding, not unlike **Montségur,** the Grail castle of the South. The ascent is no less steep and the views from the raven-haunted ruins on the summit equally spectacular.

—Glastonbury—

Map 21, ST4938

Here Joseph of Arimathea founded the first church in Britain, dedicated to the Virgin Mary, which was to become the greatest Benedictine abbey in the country. Here, says the legend, he brought the boy Jesus to tread this green and pleasant land, and here, later, he bore testimony to the Crucifixion in two cruets containing the blood and sweat of Christ. He found his final resting place by his well under Saint Mary's Chapel in the Abbey where the Wattle

Church stood. Some believe his relics repose in the sarcophagus of a different J.A.—not Joseph of Arimathea, but the silk-merchant John Allen—that forms the centre-piece of Saint Katherine's Chapel in the parish church of Saint John. A fine window above shows him bringing the cruets to Glastonbury. Here, too, in the hollow maze-hill of the Tor, Arthur descended to Annwn to bring back the cauldron of regeneration. In the reign of Henry II and Eleanor of Aquitaine his tomb and that of Guinevere were discovered in the Abbey with a lead cross, proclaiming: 'Here lies buried in the island of Avalonia, the renowned king Arthur.'

Even after the destruction of its great Abbey at the Reformation, Glastonbury remained a centre of pilgrimage and healing. Today it has become the Mecca for the New Age. Was that time already foreseen by Merlin when he laid out his Round Table as a temple to the stars—a vast zodiac imprinted naturally in the contours of the surrounding landscape—with its central point as the dove or phoenix of the Grail sign Aquarius fixed on the Tor? *(See Plate 1)*

The focus of Grail interest has now moved from the Abbey v to the Tor and the Chalice Well, which lies at its foot. Since Tennyson, its status as a Grail centre has grown remarkably. This is due, above all, to the magician, psychologist and writer Dion Fortune, who lived across the lane from the Chalice Well, and to Wellesley Tudor Pole, the founder of the Chalice Well Trust, which now preserves the Gardens and Well.

THE SAPPHIRE BLUE CUP

Major Tudor Pole (1884-1968) was a down-to-earth practical mystic and visionary who instituted the Silent Minute of prayer for salvation and peace in 1940 which the BBC marked with the chimes of Big Ben at nine o'clock every night.

He was also at the origin of a tradition concerning a chalice which he never called the Grail but rather the Cup, the symbol, as he saw it, of the new age now dawning. There are different versions of the story, but it seems that in 1906 Tudor Pole had both a vision of the Upper Room of the Last Supper and its contents and another of a chalice concealed near Saint Bride's Well in Glastonbury which resembled the chalice used on Maundy Thursday. He encouraged his sister Katherine and two of her friends, Janet and Christine Allen, to search for the Cup, which they found on the site. Does it add to or detract from the mystery of the cup and its story that it was, it seems, originally discovered by a Dr Goodchild in Italy some twenty years earlier?

Between 1906 and 1914 this sapphire blue Cup was kept in the little Oratory in an upper room at 16 Royal York Crescent in Bristol. Until 1909 the vessel was on view to the public when it was unveiled daily on the altar. From that time and before 1914 the Cup was taken to Palestine, Egypt, Syria, Constantinople, Mount Athos, **Vienna**, Budapest, Michael centres in Italy, France, Germany and Holland as well as **Iona**, where it revived sacred points all over the island. Between 1920 and 1935 the Cup once again set off on its travels all over the British Isles and elsewhere to re-potentiate holy places and objects whose power would be needed to protect the land in the dangerous times ahead. These included the Coronation Stone, itself a Grail-symbol, in Westminster Abbey, and the altars of Saint Paul's and Westminster Cathedral. From 1939 to 1943 it was in the custody of Katherine. After that it was preserved by Oliver G. Villiers who noted that it continued to have periods of rest and activity when it indicated the need to visit certain spiritual sites. Today it is still resting, and not on view, though we have held it in our hands. It is a shallow dish, 5¼ inches in diameter, consisting of two layers of glass, rough underneath, whose smooth and shining surface is studded with beautiful, blue, eight-petalled star-flowers. Its dating is uncertain—some experts consider it to be Roman work, possibly from Antioch, while others have placed it as late as the fifteenth century.

THE NANTEOS CUP

A friend told us that when, in her youth, she lived near Hay on-Wye (Map 33, SO 2342), a Grail, renowned for its healing properties, was in the possession of some neighbours, the Miryless family, who lived in a house called The Moor, 0.8km north-east of Hay. Mrs Miryless had no doubt that this was the Cup of the Last Supper. When her daughter suffered severe head injuries and her life was in imminent danger, she took the cup from its box and prayed. Within minutes the hospital telephoned her to say that the bleeding had miraculously stopped.

This, from its description and photograph, is the original Glastonbury Grail. At the Dissolution of the monasteries, Richard Whiting, the last Abbot, before his martyrdom, entrusted Glastonbury's most famous relic to his monks who carried it away to the temporary safety of remote Strata Florida (Map 45, SN 7465), a twelfth-century Cistercian Abbey, 24km south-east of Aberystwyth. When Henry VIII's iconoclastic soldiery approached the Abbey, its prior and a small group of monks set out with the Grail towards Aberystwyth perhaps hoping to take it to a sure haven across the seas. They stopped for rest and refreshment at Nanteos Manor (6.4km south-east of Aberystwyth), where the

Lord who bore the time-honoured name of Powell, that of the King of Dyfed and the underworld, bade them welcome and offered them refuge. The prior became the family chaplain and the monks found work on the estate. When the last of these was on his deathbed he entrusted the Grail to his master, charging him that the cup shall remain at Nanteos until 'the church claims its own'. It remained at Nanteos for 400 years, except when it was sent forth to people who needed its healing powers in the surrounding area. Generally it sat without great ceremony in the drawing room where the mother of a Welsh friend of ours recalled seeing it during her frequent visits to the manor.

George Powell (1842-1882) was a great admirer of Wagner and attended the first performance of the Ring Cycle in Bayreuth. Wagner almost certainly stayed at Nanteos while he was working on *Parsifal*, his final masterpiece, and his portrait hung in the beautiful music room. In 1952 the last of the Powells of Nanteos died and the cup passed to the Miryless family. It has now been withdrawn from circulation and was housed, at least for a time, in the vaults of Barclays Bank in Aberaeron. The cup is made of dark olive-wood, originally 13cm in diameter and 6cm at its base, but has been much eroded by the teeth of the faithful over the centuries, so that today one whole side is missing. Its whereabouts today are unknown to us, but there is currently a move afoot to have the Nanteos Cup returned to Glastonbury.

Flavia Anderson has produced evidence from the fourteenth-century monk, John of Glastonbury, that a crystal cross was presented by King Arthur to the Abbey. Our Lady had given it to him as a sign at the end of Mass on Ash Wednesday and it was carried in procession every Wednesday and Friday during Lent until the Dissolution of the Monasteries. Then it was presumably hidden as it was not included in the list of Abbey Treasures. Abbot Whiting was martyred on the Tor for having hidden certain treasures from the King, though this could equally well apply to the Nanteos cup as to the crystal.

—Hailes Abbey—

Map 34, SP 0530
3.2km north-east of Winchcombe in Gloucestershire off B4632

Hailes Abbey was the major shrine of the Holy Blood in England.

It was built by Richard, Earl of Cornwall, in 1251 to fulfil a vow after he was preserved from shipwreck. He was the son of King John and brother of Henry III. Named after his uncle, Richard Coeur de Lion, he gained prestige in the

Crusades, was elected King of the Romans and of Germany, and arranged a truce which gained access for pilgrims to Jerusalem. He built Tintagel Castle and was interested in his Arthurian heritage. His second wife, Sanchia of Provence, whose sisters married the Kings of England, France and Sicily, had a son, Edmund, who donated the relic of the Holy Blood for which Hailes was chiefly famous.

Richard and Sanchia were crowned in **Aachen** in 1257 by the Archbishop of **Cologne**. In Germany, either then, or at some point during the next ten years, Edmund acquired the Holy Blood relics which he distributed to Hailes and **Ashridge**. According to a chronicle, the young prince was playing in the imperial treasure-chamber when he was attracted to a golden casket, clasped with a golden chain and secured on all sides with locks. When Edmund discovered that it contained the Blood of Christ, and was hung around the neck of the Emperor when he was anointed, he would not be content until he was allowed a portion of it.

The drier account of the relic's provenance was that Edmund purchased it from Count Florenz V of Holland after it had been brought to Europe by his predecessor Count William II, having been authenticated by Pope Urban IV (1261-4), former Patriarch of Jerusalem and Bishop of Liège (see **Orvieto**).

Whatever its origins, the relic soon made Hailes one of the most important pilgrimage sites in England. By the time Chaucer wrote *The Canterbury Tales* some eighty years after Edmund's death, the Blood of Hailes seems to have become something to swear by.

> *Vengeance shal not parten from his house,*
> *That of his othes is outrageous.*
> *By Goddes precious herte, and by his nails,*
> *And by the blood of Christ that is of Hailes.*

The relic was described at the Dissolution as being contained in 'a round beryl, very securely stopped and ornamented and bound round with silver'. The container was also described at the same period as 'a crystal glass as thick as a bowl on one side and thin as a glass on the other'. The Blood only liquefied when the thinner side was exposed to a penitent in a state of grace. Of the many miracles attributed to the blood of Hailes, two concerned disbelieving priests who gorily encountered the reality of the Transubstantiation while saying Mass (cf **Bolsena, O Cebreiro** et al).

The relic was declared a forgery by Bishop Hilsey of Rochester at Saint Paul's Cross in November 1539 and destroyed. The foundation of the shrine still remains in the ruined church, near the centre of the chevet which can be seen to the left, before reaching the ruins of the monastery behind the raised grass mound, which is all that remains of the high altar. *(See Plates 2 and 3)*

The Abbey, museum and gift shop are managed by English Heritage and are open 1 April to 30 September daily 10—6; 1 October to 31 March, Tuesday to Sunday 10—4pm, telephone 0242 602398.

Further reading: Doreen Winkless' *Hailes Abbey.*

—London—

WESTMINSTER ABBEY

After the capture of Constantinople by the Crusaders in 1204 a relic of the Holy Blood was brought to Westminster and venerated there until the Dissolution of the Monasteries.

The British sacred talisman, the Stone of Destiny, can, however, still be seen in the Abbey under the Coronation Chair. According to legend it was Jacob's pillow at Bethel when he saw the ladder full of angels who link heaven and earth. Thence it was taken to Egypt, Spain, Ireland, where 131 High Kings were crowned on it at Tara, then **Iona**, Dunstaffnage and **Scone**. There Edward I seized it in 1296 and brought it to his capital.

The Sapphire Blue Cup was placed on the Coronation Stone in order to revive its powers between 1920 and 1935 (see **Glastonbury**).

The Abbey is open every day. On Wednesdays from 6-8 pm entry to Edward the Confessor's Chapel is free. This is the only time that the taking of photographs is permitted.

THE TOWER

This is where the head of Bran (see **Dinas Bran**) was buried after a remarkable journey from the west of Ireland. Bran is one of the major prototypes of the Fisher King, as his cauldron is a protograil. The Hallows of the land are still kept here, guarded by his ravens which preserve Britain from invasion.

—Peel/Isle of Man—

Map 64, SC 2484

Professor Goodrich, basing her hypothesis on *Sone de Nansai* (see Notes on the Sources), places the Grail Castle here and claims that it was re-established by Merlin and Arthur as a Christian centre.

—Penzance and Marazion—

Map 6, SW 4730

In *Perlesvaus* or *The High History of the Holy Grail* it is from Arthur's court at Penzance, the westernmost town of Britain, that the Quest for the Grail is instituted, when three damsels enter the assembly. One upbraids Perceval for failing to ask the Grail a question. The second carries a red-cross shield, like that of the Templars, which had once belonged to Joseph of Arimathea. The third has a star round her neck.

It was at Marazion, 4.8km to the east, that Joseph of Arimathea traditionally disembarked with the Holy Grail.

—Richmond—

(Yorkshire) Map 72, SD 1701

The legends of Potter Thompson, who discovered King Arthur and his Knights in a cave above the Swale under Richmond Castle, are probably distant memories of the Battle of Cattraeth (Catterick) in the early sixth century.

Here, a Celtic army from the North swooped down to attack the Angles on the plain and were wiped out to a man. As the old poet Aneurin puts it: 'None to his home returned~ Among their number was Peredur 'of steel arms' who was the British prototype of the Grail knight Sir Perceval. If any had escaped it would have been along the Swale to the high rock caves under present-day Richmond.

—South Cadbury—

Map 13, ST 6325

This is today the most favoured site of Arthur's Camelot, and an important Celtic hillfort which was not captured by the Romans until AD70. According to tradition Merlin built the great palace, whose foundations have been thoroughly excavated, in a single night. For a full description of it see our *On the Trail of Merlin*.

—Taunton—

Map 12, ST 2224

Among true Grails said to be found in Britain, Sinclair includes the bronze **Glastonbury** bowl, usually to be seen in the County Museum in Taunton, but, at time of writing, part of a new display in the Tribunal, High Street, **Glastonbury**. It was discovered in peat just outside the border-palisading of **Glastonbury** lake village, in 1893. It measures 80mm by 123mm and can hold two thirds of a litre. It is believed to be of local craftsmanship, but otherwise little is known of it for certain.

—Winchester—

(The Round Table) Map 15, SU 4729

Ancient capital of England and burial-place of her Anglo-Saxon Kings, Winchester is also the home of the Round Table. This venerable relic, which hangs in the Great Hall at Westgate, is not the original at which the Holy Grail first manifested itself to Arthur and his Knights, but a celebration of the elder chivalry, built for Henry III or Edward I, *c.* 1250-1280.

The massive circle, 5.5m diameter, made of 121 separate pieces of oak, weighs l220kg and was painted in its present form before 1522 when Henry VIII brought Charles V, the Holy Roman Emperor, to gaze on it. On it are depicted King Arthur, in the form of the young Henry, surrounded by the names of twenty-four of his Knights, the first four being Sir Gallahallt, Sir Launcelot deu Lake, Sir Gaweyn and Sir Percy Vale. The Great Hall, open daily to the public, is all that remains of the Norman Royal Castle.

Scotland

*

—Edinburgh—

(Arthur's Seat) Map 89, NT 2573

What other European capital has such a wilderness of a mountain rising in the midst of it? Arthurian connections with the men of the North, the Strathclyde Britons of southern Scotland, are now firmly established. In one account, Perceval was told to take the broken sword to the smith Trebuchet at a loch very near the Firth of Forth, surely one of the three that surround the peak. Lady Flavia Anderson hints enigmatically that the *silver tassie* may be buried there. Many people still climb **Arthurs's Seat** on May morning, the feast of Beltane, to see the sun rise.

Two major Arthurian sites, Berwick Law and Traprain Law, are clearly visible to the east, the former being particularly impressive.

—Iona—

Map 99, NM2824

An I mo chridhe
I mo ghraidh

'Island of my heart, Island of my love', was how Columba, its founder, described Iona, birthplace of the Christian Gaelic nation of Scotland and burial place of her Kings.

According to legend, the Stone of Destiny (see **London**), Jacob's heaven-sent dream-pillow, *Lia Fail*, was first brought here from Tara and thence to Dunstaffnage, **Scone** and finally London. Whatever its true provenance, and it seems most likely to have been the Pictish coronation stone, it is the most ancient symbol of sovereignty in Britain and, if the Grail is a stone, the Scottish Grail. But Iona has stones of its own—St Columba's Pillow, to be seen in the Abbey museum, and, until the nineteenth century, the black stones, near Columba's tomb, at which chiefs met to swear solemn oaths and settle disputes. They are called black because if an oath was not carried out a black doom would overcome the false swearer.

It also has a well of youth on the slopes of Dun I, and it seems that this old druidic yew-tree isle of death has become the new Tir-nan-og, the land of eternal youth and rebirth, the Gaelic Avalon, rivalling **Glastonbury** and supplanting St Kilda, Arran, Grassholm, the Isle of Man and Corvo in the Azores.

Tudor Pole (cf **Ireland** and **Glastonbury**) saw Iona as one of the three major Grail centres of the British Isles. He commissioned a wood-carving of St Michael and the dragon to be placed in the Abbey. Decades later it was attacked by a schizophrenic and hurled into the sea. One day the dragon was washed ashore and it now resides at Little St Michael's by the Chalice Well in **Glastonbury**.

Tudor Pole took the Sapphire Blue Cup of **Glastonbury** to Iona to re-potentise the sacred sites there in preparation for the isle's re-illumination under the Very Reverend Lord MacLeod of Fuinary, who founded the Iona community in 1938. This appears to have succeeded since Iona now, like **Glastonbury**, is a pilgrimage Mecca, for both the old age and the new.

—Rosslyn Chapel, Roslin—

Map 83,NT2663

O'er Roslin all that dreary night,
A wondrous blaze was seen to gleam;
'Twas broader than the watch-fire's light,
And redder than the bright moon-beam.
                    (The Lay of the Last Minstrel, Sir Walter Scott)

Sir Walter Scott is drawing attention to the mysterious glow that traditionally suffuses the stones of Rosslyn whenever a member of the Sinclair family dies. The last well-attested occurrence of this phenomenon took place five days after the outbreak of World War II when a youthful member of the family died on active service in the Royal Air Force. It is only one of many strange happenings which we were to experience and hear about in Scotland's Grail chapel.

Its construction was begun by William Sinclair, the last *Jarl* of Orkney, in 1446, when he was already forty years old, and ceased, leaving it in its present unfinished state, at his death fifty years later. This patron of craftmasons throughout Scotland and, reputedly, a grand master and adept of the highest degree, took personal responsibility for every detail of the architecture and sculpture.

Of the many mysteries he thus revealed we can mention only a few. There is the lapidary proof in the form of clearly recognizable corn cobs and aloe cactus, carved on an arch and a beam in the interior, that his ancestor, 'Prince' Henry Sinclair, had already discovered the new world a century before Columbus. Certainly around 1600, when Scottish Freemasonic Lodges were reorganised, they claimed the Sinclairs as hereditary Grand Masters of their Order from the time of Sir William.

In fact, the Sinclairs, in their various branches, were one of the most influential families in Europe from the tenth century. Marie de Saint Clair, descended from the Rosslyn branch, was married to the first independent Grand Master of the Prieuré de Sion, Jean de Gisors, after it had separated from the cognate Order of the Temple. After his death she succeeded him as Grand Master, and another Saint Clair held the title in the fourteenth century. The most recent Grand Master is the contemporary Pierre Plantard de Saint Clair. The family is thus, if one accepts the argument of *The Holy Blood and the Holy Grail,* descended from the last Merovingian monarch and is of the line of David. As Wolfram von Eschenbach points out, the Templars are the guardians of the Grail and its family, so it is not surprising to find them so well represented at Rosslyn, a bastion of the bloodline. Recent work has associated a Templar legend with the early lords of Rosslyn but as yet little substantial evidence can be produced to support this … which is not to say that there is no truth in it.

William Sinclair *the Seemly* brought back the Holy Rood either from the Holy Land or Hungary where he attended Saint Margaret as cup-bearer before her marriage to the Scottish King, Malcolm Canmore. It was a portion of the True Cross which became known as the Holy or Black Rood, impregnated with the Blood of Christ—for which Holyrood Palace and Abbey in **Edinburgh** were named. It formed, along with the Stone of Destiny (see **Ireland**, **London** and **Scone**), the most sacred part of the Scottish regalia. At the Reformation Sir William Sinclair rescued many of the treasures of the Scottish Church and Crown and hid them in Rosslyn Chapel where it is believed they are still preserved.

The crypt, which is as deep as the chapel is high, is completely walled off from the subterranean sacristy, accessible by a very worn staircase, and is filled with fine sand. It is here that many treasures may be waiting to re-emerge—the Holy Rood, a Black Virgin and Rosslyn's chiefs who

> *... uncoffined lie;*
> *Each baron ...*
> *sheathed in his iron panoply ...*

of whose presence Scott was aware. Off the sacristy is a dark, square room, once used as a prison. Judy Fiskin, the curator, invited us to enter and to feel whether there were any variations in temperature in the stones of the left hand wall. We both, independently, noticed a marked increase in heat at the same point. Is there some secret just the other side of this 1.5m thick wall playing hide and seek with us and telling us 'you're getting warmer'?

And where is the true location of the Stone of Destiny? Some say that Edward I captured a mere substitute to bring back to Westminster and that Bruce was properly enthroned on the real stone on the Moot Hill at Scone which today exhibits what it admits to be a replica.

For the other wonders of Rosslyn—its baphomet; its Hermes; its salamander; its camel; its mermaid; the supposed death mask of Robert the Bruce and an angel who bears his heart; Lucifer, falling and bound, from whose brow fell the Grail; Jesus blessing the Grail, carved in the roof; the Veil of Veronica; its multitude of Green Men and concealed Templar crosses—we must refer readers to Sinclair, Wallace-Murphy, or the evidence of their own eyes. But two monuments demand description. One is the strange Green Man, whose vacant, hollow, staring eyes greet you from the far wall as you enter and follow you round the chapel. Not only is it noticeably colder than the stones surrounding it, it seemed to have a will of its own and was remarkably reluctant to be photographed by us. On at least eight occasions both our cameras failed to function, though they had behaved perfectly normally with everything else in the chapel.

The major feature, from our point of view, is the *Apprentice Pillar*. There is an old tradition that the Holy Grail is hidden within it, though it may be that the pillar itself sums up the secret Grail teaching that the old alchemist and Rosicrucian, William Sinclair, who built the chapel, wished to convey to those who could read it aright. Viewed from one angle in a certain light it resembles a crowned and pregnant Madonna, trembling in the first stages of labour. Many before us have been struck by the optical illusion whereby it breathes, palpitates, swirls and dances, like a living being, in the play of light and shade. Visitors are struck by its evocation of the double helix phenomenon that so recently unlocked the secrets of life in DNA.

Many have compared the pillar to Yggdrasil, the Norse Tree of Life which links the different levels of the universe. Much of the nature wisdom of the old religions—Teutonic, Celtic and Greek—is encapsulated here and in the Chapel as a whole. At the foot of the pillar eight serpents seem to rotate like a carousel. Eight is the number of evolution and the law of cause and effect, as well as of perfect balance and the combined powers of sun and moon.

A legend tells us that the master mason had received a model from his patron of a pillar of great splendour. But before beginning to sculpt it he wanted to go to **Rome** to meditate further on it. During his absence his apprentice received a vision of the completed pillar in a dream and built it. When the master returned and saw the apprentice's pillar he was so enraged that he killed him on the spot. A sculpture of his face bearing a wound in the precise place where Hiram Abif, builder of Solomon's temple, was struck, can be seen on the wall watching his handiwork.

The master's own creation of this special pillar was taken to Portugal, the only other country apart from Scotland where the Templars continued to survive. It is now kept in Sintra, in a private garden, and, we are told, is even more elaborate than the one in the chapel.

Wallace-Murphy sees in the crown of the pillar the twelve constellations of the zodiac although these are not easy to discern.

We saved up Rosslyn as the last port of call on our odyssey in deference to Ravenscroft's perverse notion that the pilgrimage to Santiago de Compostela should be travelled the other way round, starting in Galicia and ending in Rosslyn. To him the seven planetary stages of the great pilgrimage that is called the Milky Way were as follows: Santiago de Compostela, the Moon; Toulouse, Mercury; Orleans, Venus; Chartres, the Sun; Notre Dame de Paris, Mars; Amiens, Jupiter; Rosslyn, Saturn.

Mrs Ravenscroft, in her late sixties, having never been on a horse before, rode all the way along this route, darkly studded by Black Virgins, from Compostela to Rosslyn. When she arrived she chained herself to the *Apprentice Pillar* in a vain attempt to force the authorities to x-ray it and discover the Grail. Later radar researches, carried out by Tony Wood and Greg Mills, operating Groundscan Radar equipment, have detected no metal object within. None of this detracts from the enigmatic glory of this ultimate Grail chapel.

Don't miss the beautiful Rosslyn Glen walk, leading through an ancient forest, seasonally rich in wild raspberries, to where the North Esk river sparkles beneath cliffs, caves with mystic carvings and the face of Old Meg, the hag, who cast her chucky~stones into the stream-bed. The air, lighter and purer the further down you go, and the healing presence of the trees and plants, help one to understand why the site was selected. The chapel itself has been likened to a physic garden in stone.

A once famous healing site in the vicinity is the well of Saint Catherine of Alexandria, herself the personification of Gnosis and patron of the Sinclairs. Her black and oily waters cured all skin diseases.

The conventional etymology of Rosslyn derives from the Celtic words *ros,* a promontory and *lin,* a waterfall, though the Sinclairs have also been pleased to see in it the red stream, signifying the Blood of Christ, which is personified in Saint Roseline, a little-known saint, much favoured by the Grail family whose name is not so far removed from Roslin or Roselin and Rosline, as it was written until the nineteenth century. Rosslyn has also been interpreted as a Stone fallen from Heaven, though Chambers' *Scottish Place Names* gives the less romantic translation of 'morass at a pool~

Perhaps the last word on Rosslyn should be left to the great Sinclair himself, who carved engrailed Sinclair crosses on the chapel walls. On a lintel next to the *Apprentice Pillar* he carved a Latin inscription which, translated, reads: 'Wine is strong, a King is stronger, women are even stronger, but TRUTH conquers all'.

Those desiring a protracted stay in the area can actually rent living quarters in Rosslyn Castle between the twin ruined towers of Robin Hood, where William Sinclair was born, and Little John, from the Landmark Trust, telephone 0628 82592.

We recommend those requiring a shorter stay to book in at the Rosslyn Inn with its four-poster beds and Routier cuisine. Telephone 031 440 2384.

—Scone Palace/Old Scone—

Map 88, NO 1123
3.2km north of Perth on A93

Scone is the ancient royal and sacred centre of Scotland. Here, the monarchs of Scotland who claimed descent from the High Kings of Ireland, and beyond them David and Solomon, were enthroned from the time of Kenneth MacAlpin, who united the Picts and the Scots in 838, to Charles II in 1651. The Stone of Destiny is known to have been kept here for 500 years. Whether it was taken by Edward I to **London** in 1296, or whether the monks palmed him off with a quickly-fabricated replica, we may never know, but if it truly sits under the coronation chair in Westminster Abbey then the ancient prophecy has been fulfilled, at least since 1603, with the advent of the Stuart Dynasty:

> *Except old seers do feign*
> *And wizard wits be blind*
> *The Scots in place must reign*
> *Where they this stone shall find.*

The Moot or Boot Hill, where chieftains from all over Scotland emptied out the earth from their brogues to symbolise their fealty to the monarch, stands opposite the main entrance to the palace. It is surmounted by a small church, the mausoleum of the Earls of Mansfield, who have lived here for 400 years. Outside the chapel is a replica of the Stone of Scone—or could it be the real thing?

If the Grail was, as Wolfram von Eschenbach believed, a stone fallen from heaven, then there is no object in these islands that more faithfully mirrors this symbolism than the Stone of Destiny (cf. **Rosslyn, London** and **Ireland**). Is it just a pleasing coincidence that Sir David Murray, the first of the Mansfield family to be Lord of Scone, was also the King's Ceremonial Cup-bearer?

Ireland

*

Ireland is the oldest source of Grail legends. The soul of the world and Mary of the Gael, Brigid, later to become, as Saint Brigit of Kildare, the foster-mother of Jesus and of Celtic Christianity, chose the Emerald Isle as the abode of the gods of light whence to beautify the world. Her father was the Dagda, the Zeus and Wotan of Eire, who possessed the earliest cauldron of nourishment and regeneration and married the river-goddess Boyne. In her lap is still to be found Newgrange or Brugh na Boinne, the inverted cup of a burial chamber where the sun penetrates each winter solstice to bring illumination and rebirth.

Ireland is the home, too, of the invincible spear wielded by Lug, the sun-god, master of all skills. He, or Nuada, planted it at Ushnagh in County Meath, where it became the ash-tree of Ireland's sacred centre at which the people of Ulster, Munster, Leinster, Connaught and Meath could meet. From here the sacred fire of Beltaine was taken to all the shrines of Ireland.

Ireland's Grail, the Ardagh chalice, can be seen today in the National Museum in Dublin. It is one of the finest examples extant of an early eighth-century chalice used for offering the Blood of Christ to the faithful. It stands 17.8cm high and is l9.5cm in diameter excluding the two handles, and is similar in design to earlier models from Byzantium and Jerusalem, though richer in amber and crystals. Other motifs include the Twelve Apostles and the animals inseparable from Celtic art.

Ardagh, south-west of Limerick, was once an important chieftain's fort and site of a monastery with a well and ash-tree, founded by Saint Molua who has been associated with the god Lug. Their feasts coincide at Lughnasa (Lammastide), the Leo harvest festival of early August.

The Grail is, by some accounts, a stone and Ireland is rich in them, from the *Blarney* stone and the Rock of Cashel to the Lia Fail of Tara. This is the six-foot (1.8m) tall monolith, known as the Penis of Fergus that roared with joy whenever a true king touched it with his foot. Another account says the Fail, once Jacob's Pillow, was taken from Tara to Scotland as the coronation stone, passing from **Iona** to Dunstaffnage to Scone and thence, plundered by Edward I, to **Westminster** (see **London**).

Tudor Pole (see **Glastonbury**), considered that the three main Grail centres in the British Isles were **Iona** (map 99, NM 2824), **Glastonbury** and Lough Erne (map 405, 14), where the Grail was reported to have been hidden for a while, presumably on the magical Devenish Island. The eighth-century Lough Erne reliquaries—one inside the other—can be seen in the National Museum in Dublin.

France and Belgium

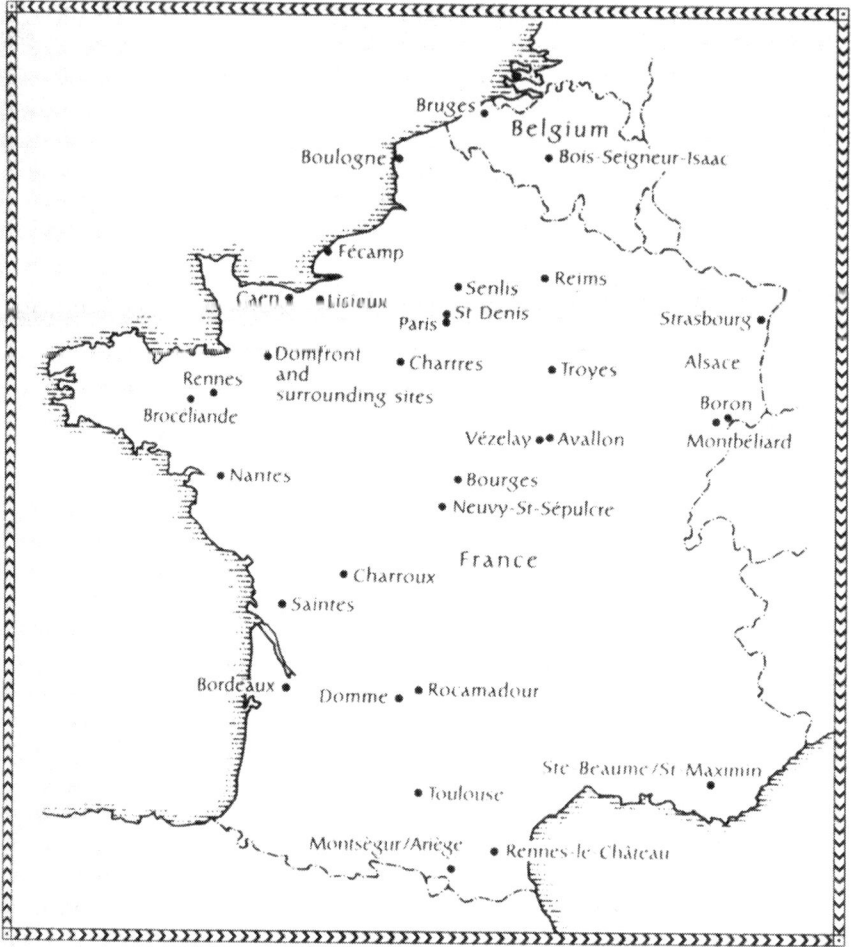

Bruges

Belgium

Boulogne

Bois-Seigneur-Isaac

Fécamp

Caen • • Lisieux
Senlis • Reims
Paris • St Denis
Strasbourg •

Domfront
and
surrounding sites
• Chartres
Troyes
Alsace

Rennes
Brocéliande
Boron
Montbéliard

Vézelay • • Avallon

• Nantes

• Bourges
• Neuvy-St-Sépulcre

F r a n c e

• Charroux
• Saintes

Bordeaux
Domme • • Rocamadour

Ste-Beaume/St-Maximin

• Toulouse

Montségur/Ariège • Rennes-le-Château

France

*

—The Grail in Alsace—

Map 242, folds 23/27 and map 62, fold 9

The main interest in this region for our purposes concerns a relic commemorating the first shedding of the Blood of Christ at his circumcision. Intriguingly, however, other elements from the Grail-legend are also to be found here. As you approach the Grail enclave of Alsace from the south along the D35 you will notice the pretty village of Itterswiler, surrounded by its vineyards. This, from its name and other indications, is the most likely home of Ither, the Red Knight (see Gurk), cousin of Parzival, who slew him in his first combat and took his armour.

ANDLAU

Three kilometres north of Itterswiler the village of Andlau seems to confirm this knightly tradition by the remarkable sculptures of two knights jousting, on the outer wall of the church. There is also an enigmatic relief of a man riding a camel, a prelude, perhaps, to the main story of the Holy Blood in Alsace. The crypt contains a skull purporting to be that of Saint Lazarus. **Avallon** and Autun also lay claim to the skull of Lazarus, who accompanied Mary Magdalen to Les-Saintes-Maries-de-la-Mer. It is an obvious talisman of Grail Christianity.

MONT SAINTE ODILE

To approach Mont Sainte Odile one should turn off to the left in Barr along the D854. Sainte Odile is the patroness of Alsace (see **Arlesheim** for her legend),

21

and in the words of Ravenscroft, the patron saint of the knights who sought the Grail. Her family bloodline flows through the royal families of Europe. The Habsburgs are direct descendants of her brother; Adelheid (see **Senlis**) married the Duke of the Franks and became the ancestress of the Capetian dynasty of France; Godefroy de Bouillon and, therefore, his grandfather, Lohengrin, are in relationship to the family as are those recipients of the Holy Blood such as Charlemagne, Baldwin of Flanders (see **Weingarten**), Thierry and Philip of Alsace (see **Bruges**), Bertha, who fought against the owner of the blood relic of **Reichenau** and Hugo of Tours (see **Niedermünster**), of whom more anon.

Odile's healing spring can still be visited on her holy mountain in Alsace by a path to the left, off the D33, that leads up to the convent. Of the many miracles attributed to her one concerned the breast of her wet-nurse—whom she buried with her own hands—which was discovered incorrupt and covered in gold like a Grail, amid the bones of the skeleton.

NIEDERMUNSTER

The memory of the first shedding of the divine blood belongs to the Abbey of Niedermünster, just below the escarpment of Mont Sainte Odile, and its legend is the most bizarre of any sacred relic. Hugo of Tours, was a servant of the Grail in the reign of the Emperor Charlemagne to whom he was close friend and adviser. He had been present at Christmas 800 in Saint Peter's when the Pope tricked Charlemagne into accepting the title Caesar Augustus. In 811 he dispatched Hugo to Byzantium to gain the recognition of the Emperor of the East. At this time, plotters at court succeeded in bringing about Hugo's downfall, accusing him of treachery and insurrection. Charlemagne had him imprisoned in a dungeon. Finally he was sentenced to death, but, first the executioner, and then the Emperor himself, found their raised sword-arms held fast by an unseen power, so that they were unable to strike the blow. Hugo was released and restored to favour by his remorseful master.

In another, more legendary but revealing account, Hugo was the thirteenth and greatest of Charlemagne's paladins, more worthy of the crown, thought the Empress, than her husband. His twelve companions, in order to save his life, were sent on a dangerous quest to perform twelve labours which included bringing back the head of Saint Lazarus (which the Scottish princess, Saint Richardis, reputedly donated later to her church of **Andlau**). The historical truth behind this legend may be that it was Charles the Fat (d. 888), husband of Richardis, who is the King in question rather than his ancestor Charlemagne. According to Stein he is the prototype of Orilus, the cruel prince, whose wife,

Jeschute, Parzival kisses on his first adventure. Whichever Charles it may be, the story that most concerns us is the gift which Hugo chose in recompense for his ill-treatment. Thus the relic of the first shedding of the Holy Blood came into his possession. The foreskin, kept in a little silver casket (cf **Charroux**), was given to Charlemagne.by Patriarch Fortunatus of 'Jerusalem' (actually Grado in Friuli) in *c.* 803.

Hugo and his wife, Aba, had a great devotion to this relic and wondered where and how it should be honoured. After much prayer he received an inspiration telling him to have a costly crucifix made of oak-wood, 1.8m high, .3m wide and two fingers deep, covered with silver leaf and showing on the reverse side to the Crucified the major mysteries of his life, sumptuously decorated with scenes from the Old Testament and a pelican feeding its young with its blood. Inside the cross Hugo placed the Praeputium Domini and several other sacred relics.

Hugo and Aba decided to leave it up to God himself where this priceless cross and relic should be honoured. Divinely inspired, they placed the cross in a chest and fastened it to the side of a camel, escorted by five trusty knights, until the animal chose to lay down its burden. It journeyed the length and breadth of France, including Paris, where it declined to stay, until it finally reached Niedermünster, the aristocratic convent under the rule of Sainte Odile (cf **Arlesheim**), where it was welcomed by the abbess and her nuns. The abbey is now a ruin, undergoing archaeological restoration, and no entry is permitted.

Whichever way you drive up towards **Mont Sainte Odile** you will come to a place called Saint Jacques where three roads meet, where the D109 from the south towards **Saint Nabor** reaches the D33 to the west, which leads up to **Mont Sainte Odile**. Stop at this intersection, on a hairpin bend, near a large private block of holiday flats which used to be the Hotel Saint Jacques. Go down the path through the forest leaving this building on your right and turn sharp right immediately past the tennis courts. In some twenty metres along a narrow path you will come to the ruins of a rectangular oratory, originally dedicated to Saint Jacques. Near here Walter Stein discovered the imprint of a camel's foot on a sloping wall. We were less fortunate, but, after much questioning and exploration we discovered the camel's hump, now well known in the locality, turned to stone on the left-hand side of the chapel, facing what was once the altar.

To reach Niedermünster retrace your steps to the main path and continue in the direction you were going, away from the road, and at the first major fork take the right-hand path downhill, which will lead you in fifteen minutes to the ruins of Niedermünster and the chapel of Saint Nicholas (closed). The great complex of **Sainte Odile**'s Hohenbourg, surmounted by its angelic statue, looms above to your left as you walk down.

The huge cross of Niedermünster, one of the most precious works of art of Carolingian France, was taken away at the Revolution and melted down in the mint at Strasbourg. The relics of Sainte Odile were rescued from her Mount by four citizens of Ottrott at this time. Was the Holy Foreskin similarly saved? The magician Vintras, who, with the Baillard brothers, founded a heretical sect based on sexual freedom at Mont **Sainte Odile** in 1837, proclaimed the Age of the Holy Spirit and was inspired by a mysterious relic which he called *la vertu* (cf **Charroux**).

The legend is charmingly preserved in two paintings. One, at Saint Nabor, the nearest village to Niedermünster, whose patron was originally Neptune—god of all living waters—can be found in the cemetery chapel, past the church, just beyond a road to the left as you travel north, behind the school. On the front of the altar the painting depicts the camel, rather tired and drooping, followed by five knights on foot, being welcomed by the Abbess of Niedermünster and her nuns. *(See Plate 32)*

The second pictorial confirmation of the persistence of the legend is in the Jesuit church of Saint George in Molsheim at the northern limit of our Alsatian itinerary, ten kilometres from Saint Nabor. Here, on the front of the altar in the chapel of the Holy Cross, a somewhat perkier camel, head held high like its fellow on **Andlau** church, followed by the knights of Saint James, now mounted, approaches Niedermünster, with Mont Sainte Odile clearly silhouetted against the skyline.

—Avallon—

Map 65, fold 16

We visited Avallon for two reasons, firstly its name and secondly the gift of the head of Lazarus, presented by the Duke of Burgundy in the year 1000 to the fourth-century church, originally dedicated to Saint Mary, but which now bears his name. This relic is no longer in the church and neither the museum authorities, nor the tourist office could give us any clue as to its whereabouts. It seems that it was divided—half being in the church of Saint Lazare in Avallon and the other half in the cathedral of Saint Lazarus at Autun where it is still preserved (but cf **Andlau**). The church, nevertheless, does retain a significant clue to the continuance of the Grail tradition in Avallon. To the right of the altar in the chapel of Saint Joseph is a rare stained-glass window showing his namesake from Arimathea in the prison where he languished for forty years nourished only by the Holy Grail. The church was reconsecrated by Pope Pascal II in 1106. It was this pope who also rebuilt the church of Saint Lawrence in Lucina, in **Rome**, and transferred there to a new altar the grill of Saint Lawrence and two phials of his blood.

Geoffrey Ashe sees Riothamus ('Supreme King'), who landed in **Nantes** from Britain with an army of twelve thousand in 468, and fought his way up the Loire Valley, as the origin of similar exploits attributed to Arthur. Like Arthur he was betrayed in his last battle and escaped with a remnant of his army towards Avallon into the territory of his allies, the Burgundians *(c.* 470).

—Boron—

Map 66, fold 8

Of the three founder-fathers of the Grail-legend, Robert de Boron has always been the least known. In **Eschenbach** the Wolfram industry flourishes; Troyes has at least a street named for Chrétien, but in the small village of Boron its greatest citizen is forgotten. Was he a knight, a clerk, or both? Was he a Burgundian from these parts or a Picard? The most we can say about him with any certainty is that his major writings, *Joseph of Arimathea,* also known as *Le Roman de l'Estoire dou Graal, Merlin* and *Perceval,* were most probably written between 1191 and 1202. He himself tells us that he wrote his stories for his patron, Gautier de **Montbéliard**, Lord of Montfaucon, who set out on the Fourth Crusade in 1202, never to return. Robert's genius and originality lie in the synthesis of the *matière de Bretagne—the* old Celtic and Arthurian legends—with the Bible and particularly the Apocryphal New Testament.

The village of Boron is 19km from **Montbéliard** as the crow flies, but by car, the easiest way is to take the D463 due east to Delle, travel north for 2km on the N19, then branch right at Joncherey and continue north on the D3 for a further 4km. Today it is a quiet hamlet on a crossroads and a stream, with a disused church, a few old timbered farmhouses and plenty of goats, peacocks and Zwetschgen-plum-trees. The only inhabitant we met was a student who lived there but knew nothing of the illustrious poet.

—Boulogne—

Map 51, fold 1

One of the oldest cults of the Holy Blood in France dates from 1104 in the church of Notre Dame du Saint Sang. The Lady of Boulogne, Ida of Ardennes, was the mother of Godefroy de Bouillon who recaptured Jerusalem and was the grandson of Lohengrin, the last Grail-King (see Ean Begg *The Cult of the Black Virgin*). Nothing now remains of the church or the relic but the Black Virgin can still be seen in the treasury of the Cathedral.

—Bourges—

Map 69, fold 1

Bourges contains the earliest pictorial representation of the Grail. A stained-glass window in the chapel of Saint Philomena in the Cathedral depicts Pope Sixtus II handing the vessel, which is now in **Valencia**, to Saint Lawrence for safe-keeping (see **Valencia**, **Huesca** and **Rome**). It is fitting that the Grail is to be found in a chapel dedicated to another triumph of the imagination, Philomena, a Roman girl martyr, who never existed. Her 'remains' were discovered in the Catacomb of Priscilla in 1802 with a phial of blood. She soon became a potent myth, venerated throughout the Catholic world until declared an un-person by the Vatican authorities in 1961. Her shrine at Mugnano, near Naples, was dismantled and her name expunged from all church calendars. Her feast, 11 August, succeeded Saint Lawrence's. (See *Plate 6*)

—Brocéliande—

The Church of Tréhorenteuc Map 230, folds 38/39
(4 km E of Néant-sur-Yvel on the D154)

In this church there is a rare depiction of the Holy Grail carried by two angels above the Round Table of Arthur and his knights. The Abbé Gillard, who became Recteur of **Tréhorenteuc** in 1942, was inspired to make of his half-ruined church a chapel of the Holy Grail. In a spirit of reconciliation he gained the co-operation of two German prisoners of war, Karl Rezabeck and Peter Wisdorff, to execute his plans. This is a true esoteric Grail church as indicated by the message on the main portal which says: 'La porte est en dedans' (the door is on the inside). Here you will find images of the Grail, the Round Table, Joseph of Arimathea, Christ as a White Hart and Morgan-le-Fay, boldly attired in scarlet, as Mary Magdalen. This marriage of Celtic and Judaeo-Christian myth is particularly appropriate here in the ancient, magical forest of Brocéliande where the kings have names like Salomon and Judicael.

If the church is shut, the key can be obtained from the sacristan, whose house is the second on the right in the courtyard behind the church, just off the main street. To obtain postcards and guidebooks, enquire at the second café on the left at the crossroads.

At Comper the Lady of the Lake raised Lancelot in her underwater palace to be the best knight in the world.

For the magical spring of Barenton, its Galician guardian, Ponthus, and the heresiarch Eon de l'Etoile, who could conjure up supernatural Grail feasts, see our *On the Trail of Merlin*.

—Charroux—

Map 72, fold 4

According to an apocryphal tradition, Charlemagne was hearing Mass in the Cathedral of the Holy Sepulchre in Jerusalem when he was granted a vision of the divine right hand blessing the chalice and placing a mysterious object on the holy vessel. A boy of angelic countenance appeared to the right of the altar and said so that all could hear: 'Most noble Prince, receive the gift of my flesh and my blood'. On the voyage back to France the Emperor died and was restored to life when the mysterious object, identified as the foreskin shed by Christ at his circumcision, was placed on his lips. According to *The Golden Legend* by James of Voragine, the foreskin was brought by an angel to Charlemagne who placed it first in the church of Saint Mary in **Aachen** before donating it to Charroux. Voragine adds that the relic in his time (1264) was to be found in the Sancta Sanctorum in **Rome** along with the sandals and umbilical cord of Christ at Saint John Lateran.

The source of the abbey's prestige and wealth consisted of seventy-five relics, exposed from 1082 in the centre of its rotunda, based, like that at **Neuvy-Saint-Sépulcre**, on the Holy Sepulchre in Jerusalem. The famous relic of the circumcision was known as *la Sainte Vertu,* (cf **Niedermünster** and **Calcata**).

There is no doubt that a cult of the Precious Blood existed at Charroux continuously from 1080, when hidden relics were discovered embedded in a wall, but it probably originated with the foundation of the Abbey in 785.

Coincy Saint-Palais asserts that it was part of the Holy Blood of **Mantua** that was the most important of Charroux's relics. Pope Leo III, who crowned Charlemagne, having consecrated Charroux the year before (799), brought together many scholars who verified the tradition concerning this illustrious relic. The Blood relic could have been given by Charlemagne to Charroux after his visit to **Mantua** in 804.

The remaining glory of the Abbey today is the octagonal, arcaded tower which once stood at the centre of the rotunda and housed the relics. To visit the ruins and the museum you must go to the Syndicat d'Initiative and take a guided tour. This we did, and came at last into the room containing the Holy of Holies, a wall cabinet in which three famous reliquaries are guarded. The problem is, which one held the Holy Prepuce? Though there is some doubt, at least in our mind, as to which of the three reliquaries contained *la Sainte Vertu*, the guide indicated that it was the second one. This seems plausible given its shape, which is perfectly constructed to contain the hooded phial, now in the church of Saint Peter in Poitiers, where it is exposed every afternoon.

The reliquaries were rediscovered when the Ursuline nuns took over the ruins of the abbey. During excavations in 1856 the builders found buried in the earth two magnificent reliquaries of silver gilt and a third of crystal, open and empty. When they opened the largest reliquary they found a small crystal flask, well hidden, with a little blackish lump in the bottom, which was believed to be the remains of the Precious Blood. This is now kept in Saint Peter of Poitiers.

Every seven years at Corpus Christi the relics are exposed for veneration at Charroux. The popular etymology of Charroux is *chair-rouge* (red flesh).

—Chartres Cathedral—

Map 60, folds 7/8

The Grail/Ark of the Covenant to be found at Chartres suggests that the Templars may be trying to indicate that they succeeded in their mission to find the Ark—perhaps, eventually, in Ethiopia. A statue of the priest-King Melchizedek shows him holding a cup which contains a stone. It was such a cup that the Cathars were reputed to venerate in the cave of **Bethléem/Ornolac** at

Ussat. A capital of the north tower depicts two strange birds drinking from a Grail cup.

On the columns of the north portal, called the door of the Initiates, are two reliefs, one of the Ark drawn by a yoke of oxen with the inscription *Archa cederis* (the Ark of the Covenant in Latin is Arca foederis, one of the titles of the Virgin Mary along with Spiritual Vessel). The second depicts a man holding a chest near a number of dead bodies above the inscription *Hic Amititur, archa cederis.* Charpentier, advised by a Latinist, suggests that the two inscriptions might be translated: 'You are to work through the Ark' and 'Here things take their course; you are to work through the Ark'.

Chartres was the sacred centre of the druidic world and home of the great Black Virgin, Our Lady of the Underworld. In its sacred architecture it contains also an important message about the Grail.

—Domme—

Map 75, fold 17

Try to approach Domme, crowded like all three-star sites, from the east by the D46 and park off the road as near as possible to the Porte des Tours, the fortified gateway to the town.

The Bastide of Domme was newly completed in 1307 as part of the fortifications along the Dordogne against the English. It changed hands a number of times during the Hundred Years War and the Wars of Religion, but it was to be put immediately to a shameful use. On the orders of King Philip the Fair every Templar commandery in France was seized on 13 of October 1307 and the Guardians of the Grail imprisoned. They were subjected to the most appalling tortures to make them confess to crimes, heresies and blasphemies of which they had been falsely accused so that the King could seize their wealth and break their power. Many, like their Master, Jacques de Molay, were killed; others, as at Domme, were incarcerated for over ten years in grim conditions. During this time they scratched on the walls of their gaol, using nails and pebbles, graffiti demonstrating their faith in Christ, the Blessed Virgin Mary and the Holy Eucharist. But there are other representations which point to their understanding of esoteric Grail Christianity. In one of these a crowned, crucified Christ has on his right the figure of Joseph of Arimathea. A cross of Lorraine rises from his right shoulder while in his right hand he holds what seems to be a funnel-shaped container near the right knee of Christ. In his left hand is a cross with a long vertical, which, at the point where it reaches the right hand and the funnel, thickens into what looks like a hollow handle in the shape of a reversed L whose bottom touches the ground at his feet. Falling towards the top of this cross is a huge spearhead drop of blood issuing from the right arm of Christ. Under his left arm is sketched a naked pregnant female figure with hands joined as if in prayer and a rod (or flute) of sorts between her arms. Is this Mary Magdalen carrying in the Grail of her womb the holy bloodline of Christ issued from the Rod of Jesse? Elsewhere the glorified Christ is shown holding the chalice of his saving blood. (For these detailed descriptions we are indebted to the sketches and texts of Coincy-Saint Palais.)

The gate-towers are locked and cannot be visited, but luckily an old man, sitting on a chair in the Place d'Armes inside the gates, confirmed to us that the graffiti were indeed still there and that if one of us stood on the shoulders of the other and peered through the arrow-slits, we should be able to see some. This we did, not without difficulty, and were rewarded by a narrow distant glimpse of some of the sketches. All our efforts at the Syndicat d'Initiative to gain entry to the towers or, indeed, any information about the graffiti, ran up against a blank wall. Someone seems to be very anxious to ensure that the Templars' secret should remain just that.

—Fécamp—

Map 231, fold 20

EGLISE DE LA TRINITÉ AND
FOUNTAIN OF THE PRECIOUS BLOOD

Centuries before Mont Saint Michel, Fécamp was the major pilgrimage centre of north-west France. Its Abbey church of the Holy Trinity ranks in size and grandeur with **Chartres** and Notre Dame de **Paris**. Clearly, there is a powerful tradition that informs these facts, but it is a tangled one in which various threads need to be unpicked.

The story begins in Jerusalem with the descent from the Cross, when Joseph of Arimathea and Nicodemus obtained permission from Pilate to bury the body of Christ. While wrapping Jesus in his shroud Nicodemus noticed dried blood round the wounds on his hands and feet and scraped some of it off with his knife, hiding the flakes in a leather glove. On his death-bed he entrusted this sacred relic to his nephew Isaac. Threatened by the Jewish religious authorities,

Isaac took refuge in the Phoenician port of Sidon where he was later warned in a dream that the Romans were about to invade Judaea. Fearing the Holy Blood might no longer be safe, he sealed it in one, or possibly two, lead cylinders and inserted them in a hollow fig tree growing next to the shore. The holes miraculously closed up to conceal the relic. One day the incoming tide uprooted the tree and Isaac helped it into the sea. He learned through a vision that it would be washed up in the uttermost parts of Gaul.

We now have to skip two hundred years to the late third century when Saint Denis was evangelising the Paris region. He sent a missionary called Bozo to preach the Gospel to the pagans of Caux in Normandy. Bozo settled in Fécamp with his wife and children who, one day, brought home two leafy branches of a tree they had found on the beach. Bozo was interested to notice that they were from a species of fig unknown in the area and planted them. He planned to bring up the remainder of the tree to his garden, but died before this could be accomplished. A mysterious stranger, a Merlinesque wise old man, offered to help his widow and children complete the project and they loaded the trunk on to a cart. This was at the place where the fountain of the Precious Blood is today—a spring that gushed forth when the trunk landed there, after its miraculous voyage, and transformed what had been a brackish tidal swamp into a rich forest. Once on the cart, drawn by a pair of oxen, the trunk gradually became heavier and heavier until the cart broke beneath its weight, halfway between the fountain and the castle, site of Bozo's original dwelling-place whose ruins can still be seen. The mysterious stranger then disappeared, prophesying that on this very site a church would be built and proclaiming that the tree contained the Precious Blood of Christ.

In the sixth century Ansegise, great-great-grandfather of Charlemagne and father of Pepin of Heristal, who murdered Dagobert II and assumed the rights of the Merovingian bloodline, was hunting a stag of dazzling whiteness, which brought his horse, hounds and huntsmen to a sudden, paralysing stop, while it slowly circled the trunk of the fig tree. Ansegise, seeing this as a sign from heaven that God wished a church built there, had plans drawn up but died before work could begin.

In 602, the governor of the region, who was to become Saint Waning, Duke of Neustria, and a close friend of the Merovingian king, Clotaire III, had a vision ordering him to build an abbey in honour of the Holy Trinity. He found the trunk and made it the centre-piece of his abbey which was consecrated in the presence of the king and the mayor of the palace in 665. According to a more exciting legend, Waning died suddenly while passing through the valley and was brought before the Supreme Judge who offered him a further lease of life on condition that he built the already long-delayed abbey. Waning entrusted it to Hildemarque, who installed three hundred nuns there.

Two centuries later, during the Viking invasion, his body was removed to safety, but no mention is made of the tree and its still undiscovered treasure of Holy Blood. In 915, Rollo, first Duke of Normandy, wishing to atone for the damage caused by his ancestors, rebuilt the church. A roof miraculously floated in from distant Coutances to crown the new building, and provide a shelter for the fig tree that had landed so long ago. In 938, during a heated discussion as to what name to give the church, an old man appeared and placed a knife on the altar, inscribed in Latin with the words 'In the name of the Holy and undivided Trinity'. He then disappeared leaving the imprint of a human foot on a stone. The stone is still preserved in the baptismal chapel near the statue of the Dormition of the Virgin. This knife is said to have been the same with which Nicodemus (see also Pisa) scraped the blood off the wounds of Christ.

Richard I of Normandy, whose mother was a daughter of the Count of **Senlis**, constructed a yet more magnificent church. During its opening ceremony on 17th June 990 some men rushed into the choir with the news that the priest of **St-Maclou-la-Brière**, Isaac, had found the wine in his chalice turned to blood at the moment of consecration (cf. **Bois-Seigneur-Isaac**, **Llutxent**, **Bolsena**, **O Cebreiro** et al.).

Here the story becomes confused. How did this blood, connected with one Isaac, become identified with the blood hidden in the fig-tree by another Isaac more than 900 years earlier? The chronicle relates that Richard I of Normandy, who had found a document giving details of the relic in the fig-tree, had the relic hidden in a pillar (cf. **Rosslyn**) near the altar of Saint Severus, in the presence of two witnesses. Many miracles of healing took place there in the following two centuries. It is reported that a manuscript was discovered during his reign, giving details of the relic preserved in the fig tree, so it is clearly *this* Holy Blood that is referred to. In the 11th Century, the families of Normandy and Flanders intermarried, which led some to claim that the Holy Blood of **Bruges** originally came from Fécamp or vice versa. Meantime all the Dukes of Normandy spent their Easters in Fécamp and were buried here.

Further evidence for continued knowledge of the relic is provided by Jean d'Avranches, Archbishop of Rouen (d. 1079), who visited the monastery in the name of the Pope and congratulated the monks that God had honoured their 46 church with some of the Blood of Jesus.

During the rebuilding of the Abbey in 1171 they found, in the remains of a pillar, attached to the high altar, the knife, the stone with the angelic footprint and the two cylinders containing the Precious Blood. From now the relic enters into the story and forms the official goal of the pilgrimage to Fécamp. A small portion of the blood was sent to Norwich Cathedral by the precentor Clement, who was present at its discovery, a relic whose fate is today unknown.

Over the next six centuries the cult flourished—with a destructive interruption during the Wars of Religion—under a surprising number of Abbots closely related to the House of Lorraine and thus the Merovingian bloodline, reputedly descended from Mary Magdalen (cf **Rennes-le-Château, Sainte Beaume, Vézelay** and **Saint-Maximin**) Even a King of Poland was Abbot from 1669-1674. The king, who was also Cardinal of Lorraine, instituted the Confraternity of the Precious Blood in 1672 and a Mass of the Precious Blood was created in honour of the relic.

In 1682 the sacristan of the Abbey wrote a description of the relic: 'In a reliquary are two tubes of lead, one inch thick, one of them three inches long and the other shorter, about two inches; both contain some of the Precious Blood. There is also a small vessel attached to a silver gilt chain in which can be seen, through the crystal, a vestige of the Precious Blood, probably taken from the shorter tube'

The disasters that befell the church of the Trinity, during and after the French Revolution, are not our concern here. A former Benedictine monk of the Abbey preserved the relic and became curé of Goderville, thirteen kilometres to the south of Fécamp, where no trace of its passage remains today. The two tubes were restored to the church of Fécamp and replaced in the splendid marble tabernacle, carved in 1505 by Viscardo, which Providentially escaped the revolutionary fury.

What still remains to be seen in Fécamp? First of all the magnificent church of the Trinity itself. In the interior the splendid tabernacle, which contains the Holy Blood, is behind the high altar, showing a carving of the Crucifixion, with two cup-bearing angels collecting Christ's blood from his wounded hands. Another angel gathers the blood pouring from his left side and a fourth one holds a vessel under his feet. (*See Plate* 7) We also noted the double chapel of Mary Magdalen and the Sacred Heart, twin symbols of the Grail.

The relic of the Holy Blood is exposed to the faithful on the Tuesday and Thursday (the feast of Corpus Christi) after Trinity Sunday.

THE FOUNTAIN OF THE PRECIOUS BLOOD (5 MINUTES' WALK FROM THE CHURCH; ASK FOR DIRECTIONS)

The little chapel of the Fountain of the Precious Blood was a pleasant surprise. It reminded us of many a Celtic Holy Well, or *jaouanc*, at which in pre-Christian times the names of the children of the locality were annually recorded at mid-summer. A few steps lead down to the spring, still drinkable from the jug provided. The well is surrounded by ex-votos attesting to its salvific force and by an invaluable sequence of paintings illustrating the whole history of the cult of the Holy Blood in Fécamp.

SAINT-MACLOU-LA-BRIERE

(Map 231, fold 20)

We came here looking for any traces of the miracle of the events on 17 June 990, when Isaac, the parish priest, while saying Mass, found the wine in his chalice transformed to blood. As luck had it the sacristan and her husband were in the church, preparing it for Easter. They told us that the original building, where the miracle occurred, no longer existed. There were, however, some interesting windows in the present church depicting the legends of Fécamp and Saint Maclou. One of them showed a sacred relic arriving from the sea. It was significant to us that the husband confirmed that the port in the background was Marseilles and that the event was said to have dated back to the same period that Mary Magdalen arrived at Les-Saintes-Maries-de-la-Mer. Here was one of the missing links we had suspected: that the arrival of the Holy Blood at Fécamp is equivalent to the penetration of Southern France by Grail Christianity through Les-Saintes-Maries-de-la-Mer, and Marseilles with the cult of Mary Magdalen.

—Lisieux—

(Map 55, fold 13G)

Sainte Thérèse of Lisieux is unquestionably the most famous and influential saint of the past century. One Sunday in July 1887, when she was aged fourteen and in the midst of her struggle to become a Carmelite nun, she had a vision. She was praying after High Mass in the Cathedral of Saint Pierre in a side chapel to the south of the high altar and was just about to shut her prayer book when she saw escaping from its pages an image of Christ on the cross. She noticed drops of blood falling from him on to the ground which no one bothered to collect. She felt that this was indeed the case—that the outpouring of divine love and suffering was largely ignored. In the ten years of her life of heroic sanctity that remained she collected those drops and transformed them into the shower of roses that she rained upon the earth as she had promised

The town was almost entirely destroyed in 1944, but the Cathedral of Saint Pierre with the ancient houses around it, Thérése's childhood home, Les Buissonets, the Carmel where she served and died and the great basilica, dedicated to her, on the hill above the town, were spared.

—Montbéliard—

Map 66, fold 8

Robert de Boron's model for the Grail-castle was here, at Montbéliard, though not the magnificent Chateau of the Württembergs that now crowns the town. It is curious, though no scholars, as far as we know, have commented on the fact, that de Boron describes this site as Mont Belyal, that is to say the mountain of the prince of darkness who, in his only appearance in the Greek New Testament, is called Beliar. De Boron is often held up as the first Christianiser of the Grail, but it should be remembered that the secret ritual, whispered by Christ to Joseph of Arimathea, belonged to an alternative, underground stream, based on uncanonical material, and that Joseph, with his collaborator, Nicodemus, was never ordained an apostle and priest in communion with **Rome**, but linked up with an earlier, Celtic tradition in **Glastonbury** (see also **Boron**).

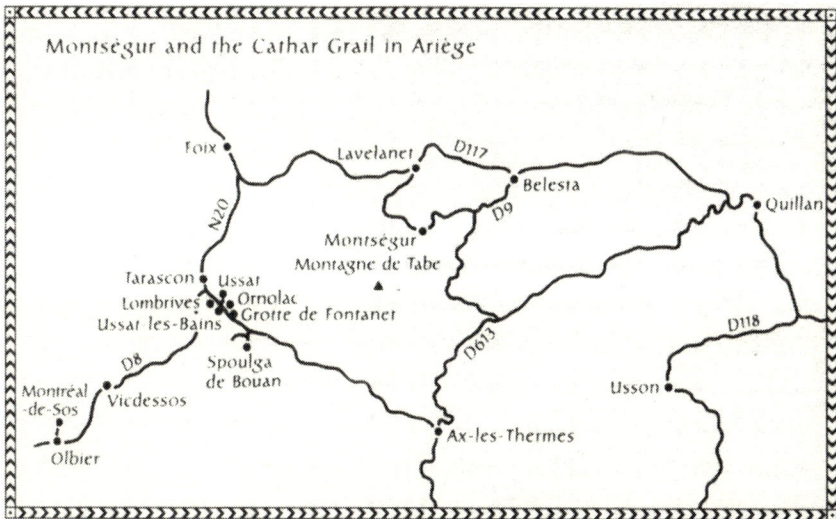

Montségur and the Cathar Grail in Ariège

—Montségur—

(Map 86, fold 5, 12km S of Lavelanet)

'Mais, apretx sept cents ans verdejo lé laurier sur Cendrum des Martyrs!'
(But in seven hundred years the laurel will be green again on the ashes of the martyrs!)

The very notion of a Grail in the foothills of the eastern Pyrenees has proved a sitting target for scholarly snipers, who point to the neglect of Catharism and Montségur itself, by historians and visitors alike, until Napoléon Peyrat wrote his *L'Histoire des Albigeois* in 1872. This, however, was scarcely surprising considering the increasingly severe repression of the history, tradition and language of Oc.

Interest in the Grail tradition in the Ariège is, indeed, very recent and stems largely from the combined interests of a schoolmaster of **Tarascon**, Antonin Gadal (1877—1962), and a number of different esoteric groups which included German Anthroposophists, Dutch Rosicrucians, the Polaires, the White Eagle Lodge and Gadal's disciple, the enigmatic Otto Rahn. Catharism lingered on in the southern part of the old county of Foix long after some Cathars escaped from Montségur. The last Parfait (Cathar priest), Bélibaste, was burnt at the stake in 1321, although the faith persisted a few more years in some remote villages such as Montaillou.

The paintings at **Montréal-de-Sos** seem to point to a genuine Grail connection in the area as do some of the graffiti at Lombrives and in other caves. There are, finally, a number of connections—place-names, Christian names, surnames and topography—which link this area not only to Wolfram's *Parzival,* which dates from the time of the Albigensian Crusade, but also to other romances with a Grail connection, such as *Huon de Bordeaux.*

It may be significant that another name for the Cathars, *patarins* or *patarini,* has possible etymological connections to *patera,* a cup, which would make them the people of the Grail. Grail itself derives from the word in Oc, *grasal,* meaning dish or, according to de Sède, a stone vessel. Finally, it has been suggested that the Grail of **Valencia** is not the true one but a replica of Saint Lawrence's cup, which Alfonso the Battler sent for safety north to the Pyrenees to preserve it from the incursions of the Almoravides (see **Huesca, San Juan de la Peña** et al). If so, this might have become the Grail of the Cathars.

Who were these Cathars whose last stronghold was Montségur, and what was their connection to the Grail? The tragedy and potentiality of human experience for them was symbolised by the *crater* or mixing bowl, the undifferentiated chaos of divine and infernal contents in which the struggle of soul-making takes place. They considered their Church to be that of AMOR, love, as opposed to ROMA with its cruel justice. The sacraments of the Roman church meant little to them—the Eucharist was the unacceptable cuisine of the unwanted Roman wife, but their own supreme initiation, the *consolament* (the ritual symbolising the connecting of a would-be Parfait or a dying believer to the spirit), was the gateway to the life of the spirit, bestowed by their beloved and forbidden mistress, the Cathar Church. Their favourite scripture was the eucharistic Gospel of Saint John, which they interpreted in an unorthodox way. Women played a priestly role in Catharism and two such Parfaites, called Esclarmonde, who set their seal on the last forty years of Montségur, became fused into one mythical character (Esclarmonde = she who enlightens the world).

At her death, released from the bonds of matter by the *cremat* of Montségur, where some 220 Cathars were burnt alive, she turned into a dove over the Montagne de Tabe and flew off, as the Grail was also to do, to seek refuge in the east. A little sculpture of a dove with outstretched wings was discovered in the ruins of the castle of Montségur in 1906 and a similar image imprinted on bronze was found on the terrace of one of the caves of **Ornolac** almost exactly seven hundred years after the capture of Montségur. It symbolises the soul of the just returning to her heavenly home. In Wolfram the dove brings down the Grail Host every year on Good Friday and at Reims it bore the ampulla, containing the holy unguent, used to consecrate the kings of France.

Montségur, whether it be Wolfram's Grail castle of Munsalvaesche or not, is one of those sacred mountains that, whatever their height, like **Glastonbury** Tor and **Montserrat**, fascinate the eye of the beholder from a great distance.

THE LAST DAYS OF MONTSÉGUR

The siege of Montségur by the forces of the King of France began in May 1243. Before Christmas of that year the Parfait, Mathieu, accompanied by Pierre Bonet, the Cathar deacon of Toulouse, with the help of accomplices from within the besieging forces, managed to escape with the money and jewels which formed the material riches of the Cathar Church. The account given by witnesses, under interrogation by the Inquisition, is understandably sometimes confusing. What seems to have happened is this: Mathieu and Pierre Bonet hid the heavier part of the treasure in a nearby wood before being guided by the men of Cambon, sympathetic to Montségur, to the best path over the Montagne de Tabe (St Barthélémy) and the relative safety of the Sabarthez. Taking with them the lighter, but evidently most precious part of the treasure, they sought refuge with Pons Arnaud de Château-Verdun whose castle, a few kilometres south-east of **Ussat**, made him the natural defender of the *spoulgas* of **Lombrives**, **Ornolac** and **Bouan**, in one of which the precious burden was placed. It was clear that this area might not be safe for long once Montségur had fallen, and the place chosen for the next stronghold was the Château of **Usson**, extremely inaccessible, near to the borders of lands which the King of France did not control. One witness reports that Mathieu was back in Montségur during February of 1244 in order to report on his mission to the leaders of the Parfaits and Pierre Roger de Mirepoix, as well as to retrieve whatever he could of the heavier part of the treasure, which he had hidden in the woods. Then he must have slipped through the siege army yet again to await the arrival of his companions at **Usson**.

Remarkably, the besieging forces had allowed the Cathars to remain in Montségur for a fortnight after they had agreed to surrender. This permitted them to celebrate for the last time the Feast of Bema, associated with the Vernal Equinox, which that year fell on 14 March.

According to witnesses at the Inquisition, on the night before the massacre, four Parfaits, Amiel Aicart, Hugues, Paytavi and another, whose name is unknown, who had hidden in a cave in the mountain beneath the stronghold, were lowered on ropes and made their escape. It seems most probable that whatever sacred objects were necessary for the celebration of the Feast of Bema—and they may have included service books, the Cathar Gospel of Saint John, a cup, a crystal for focusing the rays of the spring sun, or even the Tarot deck in which Cathar Gnosis is concealed—were removed for safe-keeping at this last moment. The Parfaits entrusted with them lit a bonfire from the summit of Bidorta to show their comrades, suffering in the flames of the execution pyre, that the mission had been accomplished.

The ruins of Montségur are as mysterious and beautiful today as ever, while the little town has reflowered (after seven centuries) into a new age Mecca like **Glastonbury**.

THE SPOULGA OF BOUAN (FORTIFIED CAVE)

Take the road to Bouan and park your car just before entering the village near the sign to 'Grotte', 200 metres from the main road.

The *spoulga* of Bouan, together with other giant caves in the area, was inhabited by the earliest Cathars in the region. It is one of the very few caves that was turned into a fortress and until 1309 was the seat of the Cathar Bishop Pierre Autier and known as the Church of Bouan. *(See Plate 9)*

The path to the *spoulga,* clearly marked on the outset, becomes increasingly elusive, but carry on until you see the sign 'Spoulga'. When we at last came upon it, it was much higher and bigger than we had imagined and well fortified. The whole of the valley was once a huge lake and invasion of the *spoulga* by boat would have been relatively easy had it not been for the fortifications. If you feel adventurous and nimble climb up to the higher levels of the cave and if you look carefully you can see the cave of Fontanet almost immediately opposite.

LOMBRIVES *(Map 86, folds 4/5)*

The caves, claimed to be the largest in Europe, are well signposted in **Ussat-les-Bains** where you can park opposite the caves in the car-park. Buy your ticket at the booth and a small train will take you up to the entrance of the cave.

In the official guide to Lombrives, whose present management are unsympathetic to Grail and Cathar connections, it is stated: 'Legend attributes the discovery of Lombrives to Roderic, the King of the Goths, who sought in the grotto an emerald table brought from **Rome** by the Visigoths' and which eventually ended up in the safe-keeping of the hermit Trevrizent (cf **Ussat-les-Bains**). Alaric, King of the Visigoths, carried away the treasure of Solomon from **Rome** to Carcassonne in 410. Procopius, the sixth-century historian, affirms that the objects of the treasury had indeed belonged to Solomon and had been taken away by the Romans from Jerusalem. After the defeat of the Visigoths by the Arabs at the battle of Jerez de la Frontera in 711 the treasure of Solomon fell into Moslem hands at **Toledo**, but not, it appears, the emerald table of Solomon (see Jaén). This was hidden in the magic love-cave of Hercules and Princess Pyrene at Lombrives where Roderic, King of the Goths, discovered in a dark corner a treasure chest containing three cups. Here we have an early connection between various forms of the Grail. To Wolfram it was the emerald fallen from the brow of Lucifer; to the French and British romancers it was a cup. In both cases it is the symbol of divine wisdom, associated with Solomon and the Queen of Sheba. In the Tarot, which, according to Runciman is the only occultist product of Christian dualism, the Three of Cups represents in its highest manifestation the inner marriage or divine love. It was just this truth that Trevrizent tried to impart to Parzival.

Napoléon Peyrat, the Protestant pastor of Saint Germain-en-Laye tells in his *Histoire des Albigeois* of 1870 of the Cathar Bishop Amiel Aicard who, having escaped from Montségur in 1244, was still preaching to the Cathar faithful in the great cathedral-cave of Lombrives as late as 1270.

Opening hours: July-August: l0am-7pm every 15 minutes; Spring holidays, June, September and every Saturday and Sunday, feast days from Palm Sunday to All Saints Day: 10 and 10.45am and from 2-5.30pm every 45 minutes; May: every afternoon; other school holidays: 3pm.

It is possible to arrange special tours by telephoning the cave's office on 61 05 98 40.

MONTREAL-DE SOS *(Map 86, fold 14)*

The cave of Montréal is not marked on the map. Coming from **Tarascon** turn left just before Vicdessos and then right to Olbier. Park in Olbier by the graveyard. Follow the path that leads from here around to the right towards the summit.

At an altitude of 1240 metres, perched on a sheer peak jutting 600 metres towards the heavens, Montréal-de-Sos was one of the most powerful castles of the Sabarthez, never taken until Richelieu ordered its destruction in the seventeenth century.

Beneath the last remaining wall of the castle is a cave with two entrances or exits. On the wall of the cave a remarkable painting was discovered in 1932 by Joseph Mandement, president of the Syndicat d'Initiative of **Tarascon**, and two friends. It shows a lance, a broken sword, a solar disk, many red crosses (as worn by the Templars) and a square panel (40cm by 40cm), rather like a table-cloth. It has an outer part with twenty crosses—eighteen white and two red, eleven Saint Andrew's and nine Greek—on a black background. An inner square contains five tear-shaped red drops of blood and five white crosses. If we take the central square as the *taillover* (dish) described by Chrétien de Troyes, we have here all the elements carried in the Grail procession. Here was the missing link betweeen the Cathars in the last strongholds of Languedoc and the Holy Grail. (*See Plate 8*)

Another missing link between Cathars and the Grail is provided by the Templars who, historically, refused to crusade against the first and, according to Wolfram, were the guardians of the second. They had a major commandery at Capoulet-Junac between **Tarascon** and Montréal-de-Sos.

Montréal-dc-Sos seemed so important that we decided to enlist the help of our friends in the region, Roger and Gigi Rieu, mountaineers and great travellers. We climbed a narrow path, much overgrown, leading up to the battered remnants of the castle of Montréal. We were glad we had the Rieu's spaniel, Emir, with us, as, seeming to guess what we were looking for, he darted off down to the right on an even narrower path. We followed him through very prickly shrubs on an increasingly slippery path with only Emir's bark to guide us until eventually we reached the first entrance to the cave where he stood, triumphantly, on the threshold of a tunnel leading into the mountain. Pot holing by torchlight was messy and painful but revealed nothing spectacular. Round the next bend we found another entrance guarded by an iron grille and we knew we had arrived at our destination. It was possible with some difficulty to squeeze round the side of the railing and observe what was left of the famous Grail mural. We could still discern in faint and faded outline all that was described in a report in La Dépêche shortly after the painting's discovery. Clearly it has suffered from exposure to the elements and the depradations of sightseers during the past sixty years.

Some writers have seen Montréal-de-Sos as the Grail castle of Amfortas and these subterranean galleries, which are almost all that remain of it, as chambers of initiation into the mysteries of the Grail. Déodat Rochet, the doyen of Cathar studies, thought Montréal a more important Grail centre than either Montségur or **Ussat-Ornolac**. What struck us particularly was the arrangement of the blood-drops on the *taillover*. These, sometimes counted as five, sometimes six, reminded us forcibly of the corporal with its drops of precious blood which we had seen at **Llutxent**.

TARASCON-SUR-ARIEGE *(Map 86. Folds 4/5)*

Little remains today of the huge castle of Tarascon in whose shadow the last Cathars could seek protection. Until 1287, when the natural dam it commanded burst, the citadel denied access to all invaders from the south seeking to force the Ariège and the great lake it formed. This lake provided easy access by boat between the *spoulgas* and Cathar communities on both sides of the valley. Within the still-standing ramparts of Tarascon, above the gateway to the inner town, is the Museum of Tarascon in the Porte d'Espagne which preserves many items of interest to those seeking information about the Grail and its Cathar connections. It also honours the memory of a remarkable man who popularised the Cathar Grail, Antonin Gadal. His many books on Cathars, druidism, the Grail and other subjects, are on sale in the small museum. As it says in the explanatory leaflet, you will find here the symbols of the Cathar doctrine of love, including the chalice of the Holy Grail that symbolises self-realisation But the greatest treasure we found here was the manuscript text of

Le Saint Graal et le Précieux Sang by Coincy Saint-Palais, though it was to be some months before we could track down a copy of it.

The Museum of Tarascon is open daily from 10-12 and 3-5. However, it is advisable to telephone first. Telephone 61 05 81 57.

USSAT-LES-BAINS/ORNOLAC/BETHLÉEM *(Map 86. folds 4/5)*

To reach Ussat-les-Bains turn off the N20 across the Ariège and the railway-line or take the D23 from Tarascon on the east bank of the Ariège, direction Ussat and Ornolac

GROTTE DE BETHLEEM

About 275m from the crossroads, park and information centre in Ussat-les-Bains, heading south towards Ornolac you will see on your right a pension called Maison Hillaire Conte. Almost Opposite, on the left-hand side of the road, is the steep path leading up to the Grotte de Bethléem on the flank of the Holy Mountain. The *spoulga* (fortified cave) is difficult to see until you come almost up to it. Push through the wooden gate surmounted by a black five-pointed star inscribed 'Bethléem—Sanctuaire Cathares', and you will find yourself inside the first of the three stages of Cathar initiation, represented here as a walled court-yard. Nothing now remains of the castle built into the cleft of the rock to which the path you are on would have led. To the right, another path leads up to the Grotte de Bethléem where the Perfect presided over the initiation ceremonies of the Grail in which candidates for the ultimate status of *parfait* received the *con-solamentum.* Entering that cave today through the arched doorway, the first thing that strikes one is the presence of a dolmen, most unusual in such an indoor setting. It rests on three round stones and gives the impression of a structure devised much later than monolithic monuments familiar throughout western Europe. Another large granite 'altar' lies as a stepping-stone beneath the entrance, and immediately to the left in the wall is a niche which is said to have contained the Holy Grail. Less clearly defined, on the rear wall, is a pentacle, some 30cm deep, with handholds and toeholds, which is believed to be a Cathar symbol that played a part in the final initiation ceremonies.

MONUMENT OF GALAAD

Continue south towards Ornolac and take the first turning suitable for cars on your right. In less than 90m you will come to a square with an iron fence enclosing a circle of eleven standing stones of unequal height with, in the centre, a square stone structure, symbolising Galahad, the Grail-King. The French name, Galaad, surmounting the gate, is also a felicitous anagram for A. Gadal, the populariser of Cathar Grail studies in this area.

GROTTE DU FONTANET

To find the grotto go along the road to Ornolac. When you come to the village square just outside Ornolac, don't turn left into the village but carry straight on until you come, after approximately 1.6km, to the end of the rough road where there is a parking area. From here a path leads straight up and then to the right along the rock wall. Keep following this path until you come to the double cave which lies more or less opposite the *spoulga* of Bouan.

> *gein Fontan Ia salvatsche ez gienc ...*
> *der kiusche Trevrizent da saz ...*
> *diu verholnen maere umbe den gral.*
> *(Then he trotted towards Fontane Ia salvatsche ...*
> *There dwelled the pious Trevrizent ...*
> *From him Parzival is now to learn the secrets of the Grail.)*
>   (WOLFRAM VON ESCHENBACH)

The site in question here is none other than the cave where Parzival was initiated into the mysteries of the Grail by his uncle, the hermit Trevrizent (but cf **Ptuj**), who in Wolfram's account is very like a Cathar Parfait. Some say the grotto in question is that of l'Hermite on the Holy Mountain of Ussat beyond Bethléem in the direction of Ornolac. But most investigators place it in the Grotte du Fontanet. The fountain had dried up during the very hot summer that we were here.

The first thing that struck us on our entry into the cave was the extraordinary luminosity both of the stalagmites and of the small round stone-shapes, embedded by constant dripping in the surface. This is indeed a rich backcloth upon which to let the imagination run riot on the host of images—all sorts of faces, sea monsters, sacrificial altar stones and dismembered limbs—that emerge from the darkness. At the far end of the cave, glowing crystals seem to beckon one ever further in, but an iron grille prevents deeper penetration. Surely Merlin's crystal cave was much like this.

USSON *(Map 86, fold 16)*

Immediately south of Usson-les-Bains, marked as Château. Carte de Randonnées 9, 580/50

Professor Markale, no enthusiast for the Cathar Grail, considers that, if the Holy Grail had been anywhere in the Ariège, Usson (most of its story is told under Montégur) is where it would have been. Once a magnificent defensive citadel, it today stands as a romantic ruin, crumbling and overgrown. From the eleventh century the castle belonged to the Alion family who were strong supporters of the Cathars. One member, Esclarmonde, was the niece of the great Esclarmonde de Foix (see Montégur). *(See Plate 10)*

Pierre Roger Mirepoix, one of the two commanders of Montségur, who had been instrumental in arranging the flight of the four Parfaits who carried to safety the treasure of Montségur, left for Usson immediately after the capitulation of the Cathars. So, it seems that after Montségur all roads led to Usson which still, for a short time, remained a place of refuge.

—Nantes—

Map 230, folds 54/55

Nantes, the largest town in Brittany and once its capital, had the oldest, largest and finest cathedral in Gaul until the Normans destroyed it in 843. In the middle of the fifth century the most probable historical model for King Arthur as a figure of importance in continental Europe, Riothamus, landed here from Britain with an army of twelve thousand men to be betrayed and beaten, seeking a final refuge on the road to **Avallon**. To Wolfram, Nantes was Camelot.

—Neuvy-Saint-Sépulcre—

(The Jerusalem of France)
Map 68, fold 19

A church is known to have existed on the right bank of the Bouzanne at Neuvy at the beginning of the eleventh century, dedicated to Saint James the Great, and a chapter of priests serviced this staging-post on the road from Vézelay to Santiago de Compostela. From 1079 it was attached to the Basilica of the Holy Sepulchre in Jerusalem.

Pilgrimages to the Holy Land were a hazardous matter, certainly before the First Crusade, but when contemporary eyewitnesses reported that a rectangular edifice had been added to the rotunda in Jerusalem, Neuvy straight away set about conforming to its chosen model. It was to be another two centuries until the round basilica, unique today in France, was to receive the relic which enhanced its claim to be another Holy Sepulchre. Cardinal Odon or Eudes of Châteauroux (1198-1273), a native of these parts, consecrated the High Altar in 1246. In 1254, during a visit to the Holy Land, he sent to the prior of Neuvy a fragment from the tomb of Christ and, more significantly, three drops of the Precious Blood in the form of coagulated tears without any admixture of water or earth. The relics were placed in a chest in a cave, representing the tomb of Christ, in the centre of the rotunda where an altar now stands. They survived many dangers from war and bigotry until menaced by the French Revolution, whose partisans were particularly strong in Neuvy. The sacristan, Jean Blondeau, entered the cave in 1794, and, opening the chest, took out the crystal tube containing the precious drops and poured them onto a corporal which he folded and hid behind a stone. He replaced them in the empty tube with three little balls of stewed fruit-juice mixed with dust and put everything back in its place. The revolutionaries, once they had desecrated the altar, were delighted to find that the relics had been nothing but a hoax all along and proclaimed the fact widely. But the last laugh was with Blondeau who, with the return of better times and the priests, divulged the truth, and the people once again venerated the relic with joy. On 24 April 1805 the Archbishop set up a commission of inquiry which confirmed the authenticity of the rediscovered treasure. In 822, however, during a procession to celebrate a thousand years of Neuvy, it was noticed that there were only two drops in the phial and the third has never been found.

We felt particularly blessed in our encounter with the present Abbé of Neuvy who patiently answered all our questions and agreed to a photo-opportunity in the courtyard of his presbytery, holding the Holy Blood, in its fine twenti-eth-century reliquary, donated by a pious Belgian family. A kneeling angel is depicted, bearing his precious burden, on a three-tiered plinth. *(See Plate 4)*

The relic is exposed for public veneration on the Sundays following 13 May and 9 October, the last Sunday in August and, above all, Easter Monday, when there is a solemn procession through the streets of Neuvy *en fête*.

Devotion to the Precious Blood for every day is fostered by the unusual red chaplets which can be obtained in the church and blessed by the curé.

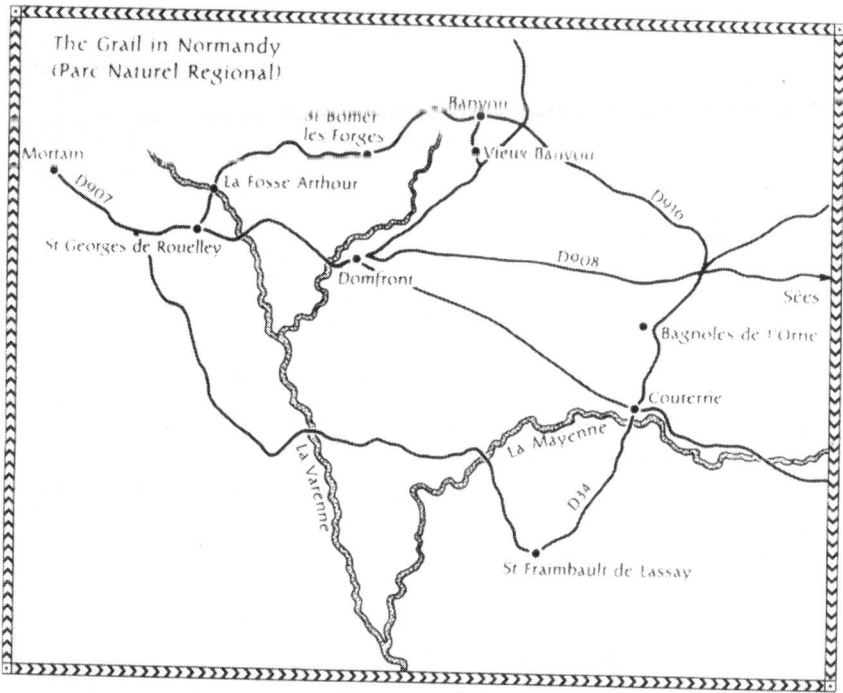

—The Grail in Normandy—

(Parc Naturel Regional)
Domfront (Map 231, fold 41)

Domfront, beloved city of the Plantagenets, was where Eleanor of Aquitaine gave birth to two daughters and held court for poets and bards.

The church, variously called Our Lady under the Water or Our Lady on the Water, to the south of the town, stands on the banks of the Varenne, a river notable for its sudden floods. It was here that King Bagdemagus made a narrow bridge between the two banks, almost 2m under the surface. This cruel passage was called the 'Bridge under the Water', by which the Grail-knight Gawain (or possibly Lancelot) crossed into the kingdom of Gorre in search of Guinevere, kidnapped by Meleagant. A strange impression of how this bridge might have looked is afforded by the wooden washhouse, the floor of which could be raised or lowered by pulleys, according to the level of the river. The remains of the ancient ford can still be seen beside the chevet. We contemplated it over a cider from the terrace of the bar opposite where we met a troubadour from Glasgow.

LA FOSSE-ARTHOUR *(Map 231, fold 40)*

From Domfront take the D907 to Rouelle and follow the rather rusty signposts to La Fosse-Arthour. Park by the Vieille Auberge (excellent local perry) and walk upstream to a gorge where the falls of the Sonce reveal a flat stone known as the *Bed of the Lovers*. In the cliff on the far side is the Queen's cave, while the King, with whom she trysted, lived in a hollow high up in the cliffs on the near side.

Who is this royal couple? Local tradition relates an unknown tale of Arthur and Guinevere. The King and Queen retired to spend their declining years in this idyllic wilderness, but Arthur came under the spell of the water nymph who was the spirit of the place. He was forbidden to visit the Queen until after sunset. He broke the interdict, and while he was wading across to the bed of the lovers the fairy unleashed the flood-waters of the Sonce and swept Arthur into a bottomless abyss. Guinevere, witnessing his tragic fate, hastened to share it by leaping in after him. For many years after two white ravens nested in the cliffs. The peasants who watched them soaring sadly over the dales blessed them, for they protected their crops from other birds, until one evening they flew off to the western horizon and were never seen again.

The memory and name of Arthur linger on in the charming hermitage of Saint Ortaire, 1.2km west of Bagnoles-de-l'Orne on the road to Saint Michel.

MORTAIN *(Map 59. fold 9)*

The Abbaye Blanche is situated at the north-west exit of the town on the D977, direction Vire. It has been identified with the White Abbey founded by her ancestors where Guinevere took refuge with the nuns. Beroul, the author of the twelfth-century *Roman de Tristan,* was a native of Mortain and a member of the court of Henry I Beauclerc, the King of England who loved Domfront.

Also at Mortain, in the church of Saint Evroult in the centre of the town, there is a sacred object which Professor Payen considers may have served as a prototype for certain descriptions of the Grail. It is a seventh-century Irish brazen beechwood casket like a little Ark of the Covenant, covered in runic inscriptions and images of human and angelic figures (cf **Oviedo**).

SAINT BOMER-LES-FORGES *(Map 231. fold 41)*

From Vieux Banvou go into Banvou itself and take the D56 to Saint Bomer-les-Forges.

Saint Bomer is traditionally derived from Bagdemagus, king of Gorre, who was guardian of the marches for King Arthur, and who was killed by Gawain. His 'tomb', a remarkable Merovingian sarcophagus, is the major site of interest in the locality.

From Saint Bomer take the D54 direction Tinchebray and turn left at the village of L'Epine-l'Orbière on the D217 direction Lonlay-l'Abbaye. After about 3km you will come to the hamlet of la Thomassière which is not marked on the map or on the road. You will recognize it by a small *calvaire* on your right, before the crossroads. Some 45m to your left, you will see on a mound what seems to be a stone Grail rising out of the field adjacent to the farm. On closer inspection, it reveals itself as a large sepulchre (a man of 2.3m can lie in it comfortably), hewn from the living rock and standing on its own with no sign of a surrounding necropolis. Lancelot once rode past it and read the inscription on the tomb. Bagdemagus was the father of the felon knight, Meleagant, who abducted Queen Guinevere, Lancelot's love. The kingdom of Bagdemagus was Gorre of which Gorron, to the south-west of Domfront, is the only toponymic remnant in Normandy.

SAINT FRAIMBAULT-DE-LASSAY *(Map 231, fold 41)*

In the town centre of Lassay turn right and almost immediately left on the D33 towards Javron. The first turning to the left outside the town is the D242 to Saint Fraimbault-deLassay. At the top of the hill, in the centre of the village, you will see the twelfth-century church on your left.

Here is the heart of the Lancelot/Saint Fraimbault tradition and the chief goal of the Grail-quest in Normandy. If Lancelot, knight of the Round Table, seeker of the Grail and father of the Grail-King Galahad, is somehow the same as Saint Fraimbault, as the traditions suggest, we need to examine the evidence.

René Bansard, in whose honour *La légende Arthurienne à la Normandie* was written, sets out the parallels:

FRAIMBAULT DE LASSAY:

- His name means the lance of the lake.

- He is the son of a king (in fact the Count of Auvergne).

- In his youth he flees the palace for the monastic life. His father tries to retrieve him but water from a cave, in sudden spate, miraculously conceals him.

- He becomes friendly with Ernier (see Vieux Banvou), a monk of the Pays d'Erne (Payerne).

- He asks a carter to bring him some stones. Deceitfully the man replies that he is carrying a corpse. God punishes him by making this true.

- He lives until 570.

- He spends his life in the monastic state.

- He dies in a hermitage (Montgermont, near Saint-Fraimbault-sur-Pisse) some distance from his own monastery, the mother-church of Lassay, to which his body is brought back.

- He is at once honoured as a saint.

LANCELOT DU LAC:

- His name means the lancer of the lake.

- He is the son of a minor king (Ban).

- Shortly after his birth he is carried away by a fairy to the bottom of a lake. His mother is powerless to get him back.

- The regent of his father's kingdom is called Leonce de Payerne.

- One day he hails a carter and mounts his cart. The next day he sees a cart with a corpse in it.

- He is still alive in 546.

- Towards the end of his life he becomes a monk.

- He dies in a distant hermitage; his body is brought back to the mother-church of Joyous Garde.

- His tomb is at once considered as that of a saint.

As you enter the churchyard turn left and in the north-east corner of the exterior wall you will find inserted the tombstone of Saint Fraimbault-Lancelot of the Lake, indicated by a sign on the ground beneath. If you examine it closely you will be able to make out a chalice and what seems at first to be a Templar cross, but is in fact a trefoil or club, as in our modern playing-cards. This may be significant, because in the French deck, where the court cards are named, the knave of clubs is called Lancelot.

In the interior of the church to the left before the choir is a statue of Saint Fraimbault with a spade and a book, standing in a niche on top of the sanctuary which preserves his head. His body was transferred to Senlis, and is still to be found in the church dedicated to him there. The observant visitor will not fail to notice some Templar crosses. Further lapidary evidence for the importance attached to Lancelot in Normandy is a carving on a capital of Saint Pierre in Caen of Lancelot crossing the sword-bridge.

SEES *(Map 231, fold 43)*

The bishopric of Sées includes most of the Lancelot country of Normandy. In the magnificent cathedral, now undergoing extensive restorations, we were intrigued to see a window representing Longinus (see Introduction and **Mantua**) as a knight in full armour on a white horse piercing the side of Christ with his long spear, for all the world as if he were Lancelot himself and indeed their names are one and the same (lonche in Greek = lance).

V1EUX BANVOU *(Map 231. fold 41—unmarked)*

At La Ferrière-aux-Etangs take the D21 direction Dompierre, and in 2km turn right towards Vieux Bourg (cf Banvou). Just after a crossroads you will notice on your left the chapel of Saint Ernier and Saint Joseph with its many large yew trees.

Of all the sites in France, this, the capital of King Ban, is the most likely to have been the birthplace of Lancelot, though nothing remains but some low remnants of drystone walls along the edge of the fields across the small river behind the chapel. The Prose Lancelot situates his home in the marches of Gaul and Brittany and, in fact, the boundaries of the bishoprics of Maine, Sées (Gaul or later Normandy) and Dol (Brittany) meet exactly here. It was said of Lancelot that he spoke the language of Gaul when he came to the British-speaking court of King Arthur.

The church is closed, but one can climb the ancient tombstones, which serve as steps, to look through a grille to the various statues, including a fifteenth-century Saint Ernier. There was a notable pilgrimage to his grave until the ninth century when his body was translated to Beaune to escape the invading Normans.

We picked an enormous bunch of mistletoe from a rotting apple tree in honour of the druids and of the great lover, Lancelot.

—Reims—

Map 56, fold 6

From the time of Clovis, first Merovingian Christian King of the Franks, French monarchs were anointed in the cathedral of Saint Rémy with chrism kept in a dove-shaped vessel. Until the bombardments of 1914 there was a remarkable statue on the south façade of the transept showing a *female* figure, symbolising the church, carrying a chalice in her right hand and a spear in her left.

—Rennes-le-Château—

Maps 235, fold 47 and 86, fold 7
About 18km south of Limoux off D118

No modern guide to the Holy Blood and the Holy Grail would be complete without a reference to Rennes-leChâteau. Its claim to fame rests on the hypothesis that the Blood and the Grail are united (sang réal from which sangreal is derived = Royal Blood) in the descendants of Jesus Christ and Mary Magdalen. According to this theory they became the founders of the Merovingian dynasty of French kings, the last of whom, Dagobert II, was assassinated near Stenay on the present Franco/Belgian frontier in 674. His son, Sigisbert IV, was taken to safety at Rennes-le-Château, the centre of the remaining Visigothic territory in France, where his mother, Giselle de Razès, came from. The story is a fascinating one and can be read in *The Holy Blood and the Holy Grail* by Baigent, Leigh and Lincoln. The symbolic decoration of the church, unique and bizarre, lends weight to the three authors' hypothesis. It is certain that the dedication of the church to Saint Mary Magdalen is very ancient and that many paths—Celtic, Visigothic, Jewish, Frankish, Templar and Cathar—meet here. Another hypothesis places here the sex of Isis, that Holy Grail in which the arcane substance of the alchemists is to be found, the extremities of the goddess stretching from the Nile to the Canary Islands.

—Rocamadour—

Map 75, folds l8 and 19

We knew Rocamadour well from earlier researches (E. Begg, *The Cult of the Black Virgin*) without having paid much attention to its qualities as a Grail centre. We were alerted to this by the statement in Atienza's *Guía de Ia España Griálica* (page 160) that 'the Holy Chalice brought from Caesarea by Joseph of Arimathea landed in Marseilles and was taken from there to Gallia Narbonensis (the Narbonne region) where it was kept for centuries at Rocamadour until the eighth century ...' Amadour, the Holy Lover, was born in Lucca and re-emerged as the diminutive publican Zacchaeus, who climbed a sycamore to witness the entry of Jesus into Jericho and became his host for dinner. He was also the husband of Veronica, the woman cured by Christ of an 'issue of blood', who wiped his face with her napkin on the way to Calvary and found his image permanently imprinted on it.

So what should Grail-seekers look for today in Rocamadour? Above all there is the ancient Black Virgin whose fame was at its height in the twelfth and thirteenth centuries when the Grail was most in honour. The multitude of saints and monarchs who paid homage to her included, in 1172, Eleanor of Aquitaine. The sword of Roland, Durandal, a suitable masculine companion to the Grail, is still venerated in the cloven rock above the chapel of the Black Virgin, though now out of reach of all the brides who sought fertility by its touch. According to legend the dying Roland, ambushed at Roncesvalles in the Pyrenees while commanding Charlemagne's rearguard, hurled the sword with all his dying might lest it fall into the hands of the foe, and it landed in Rocamadour. Of the passage of the Grail, however, we could find no traces. *(See Plate 5)*

It is the site itself, originally just a cave halfway up a sheer cliff-face, that makes Rocamadour a castle of the Grail, ever virgin in its renewals. Before the Christian hermits; before the community of female warriors worshipping Artemis; before the human sacrifices in a cavern to dark Sulevia/Cybele; before the druids; before the builders of the megaliths, Rocamadour was the meeting place of the sun-god and the earth-mother, ever bringing forth the miracle of birth, death and rebirth from her womb of night.

Sainte Baume/
—Cave of Mary Magdalen—

Map 84, fold 14

After landing at Les-Saintes-Maries-de-la-Mer (near Marseilles) with her sister, Martha, her brother, Lazarus, Saint Maximin, the first bishop of Aix, and other important figures, Mary Magdalen climbed up the valley of the Huveaune to the cave in the heart of the sacred druidic forest of the Ligurians. Here she spent the last thirty years of her life in penance and contemplation. She brought with her a phial of the Precious Blood of Christ, now at Saint-Maximin, where her tomb has been venerated since the early fifth century, though some of her relics have been returned to Sainte Baume. Maître Jacques, one of the builders of the Temple of Solomon and much revered in Masonry, was, according to tradition, murdered at Sainte Baume and buried in the grotto of the Magdalen.

—Saint Denis—

Maps 56, fold 11 and 101, fold 16

The cathedral is the burial-place of the Kings and Queens of France, and repository of some notable relics, including the head of San Pantaleón (cf **San Pantaleón de Losa** and **Ravello**) and a fragment of the Spear of Longinus, transferred here from the Sainte Chapelle at the French Revolution.

Waldo, the ninth-century Abbot of **Reichenau** (qv) and a Grail-bearer, became Abbot of Saint Denis. His tomb here was greatly honoured, but the mystical Grail school of Christianity he founded here fell out of favour. Charlemagne's biographer, Einhard, writes him out of history, though he left his own image on the bronze doors of Saint Denis which he made. Note the carvings on one of the porticoes of eight maidens bearing chalices.

The great engraved crystal of Saint Denis, possibly used for liturgical fire-making ceremonies and, in the view of Flavia Anderson, therefore a Grail, can now be seen in the British Museum.

Saint Denis walked here, to what was then only an open field, after his execution on Montmartre, with his 'head tucked underneath his arm' until he finally collapsed. The Merovingian kings subsequently had to build the Benedictine abbey on this spot in order to cope with the flood of pilgrims, and made it the richest and most famous in France.

Eon de l'Etoile, the charismatic twelfth-century Gnostic leader from **Brocéliande**, died here, having been charged with heresy before the Pope at **Reims**.

—Saint-Maximin—

Map 84, folds 4,5

After Mary Magda!en's thirty years of penance in the mountain cave of **Sainte Baume**, angels told her that her deliverance was approaching and carried her to the hermitage of her old travelling companion, Saint Maximin, near the Aurelian Way. He gave her Communion, after which she died. He embalmed her body and placed it in a magnificent mausoleum in a cave. In about the year 400 Saint Cassian, and some monks from the monastery of Saint Victor he had founded at Marseilles, built a path and some steps to make the tomb accessible to pilgrims. During the Saracen incursions of 716 the entrance to the crypt was covered by earth and stones and the remains of Mary Magdalen were placed for greater safety in the sarcophagus of Saint Sidoine, one of the four which contained relics of the early Christian saints of Provence.

In the eleventh century **Vézelay** claimed to possess Mary Magdalen's body despite the protestations of the Bishop of Autun, and it became the centre of a cult which spread to hundreds of Madeleines throughout Europe. Nevertheless, the memory of the presence of Mary Magdalen at Saint Maximin was not lost, and in 1279, under the direction of Saint Louis' nephew, Charles II, future Count of Provence, the crypt was excavated and the tombs discovered. The body of the Magdalen was unmistakable from the divine odour it exuded, the uncorrupted tongue with a sprig of fennel growing from it and the patch of fresh, rosy skin below her left eye where Jesus had touched her at his resurrection, during the *Noli me tangere* episode in the garden.

One of the major relics to be rediscovered was an alabaster flask containing the Blood of Christ collected by the saint at the crucifixion. Every Good Friday after the reading of the Passion the blood liquefied and bubbled. This phenomenon, known as the Holy Miracle, occurred as late as 1876, though, apparently, the relic is no longer displayed, but her tomb can be seen in the crypt during normal opening hours.

—Saintes—

Map 171, fold 4

According to *The Oxford Dictionary of the Christian Church*, Saintes ranked with **Bruges**, **Ashridge**, **Hailes** and Beirut as a centre of devotion where the Precious Blood was venerated. The director of the studies section of the municipal library in Saintes, though very interested in our inquiry, has not yet been able to furnish any further information.

—Senlis—

Maps 56, fold ll and 106, folds 8/9

The body of Saint Fraimbault/Frambourg, who has been identified with Lancelot, was transferred in the tenth century from **Saint Fraimbault de Lassay** to Senlis. His body is still venerated in the crypt. **Saint Frambourg** was a Chapel Royal, founded by Adelaide, the Queen of Hugh Capet, at the end of the tenth century, to house the body of the fifth-century saint and was rebuilt in the twelfth and thirteenth centuries. In 1973 Georges Cziffra, the great Hungarian pianist, took over the church, by that time a garage, and converted it into the Auditorium Franz Liszt 800 years after the reconstruction of the church by Louis VII, first husband of Eleanor of Aquitaine, and the publication of Chrétien de Troyes' *Lancelot*.

The relics amassed by Queen Adelaide and her successors, especially Louis VII, were remarkable. They included, apart from Fraimbault/Lancelot, Bomer/Bagdemagus (cf **Saint Bomer**) and other saints of Maine, Saint Bertha of the Big Foot, mother of Charlemagne (d. 783), a Merovingian princess from Laon, who by her marriage legitimised the new Carolingian dynasty. Adelaide must have felt a certain affinity with her, as the first Queen of a new dynasty who brought in her dowry the rights to Aquitaine, which two centuries later Eleanor was to bring first to Louis VII of France and then to Henry II of England.

The relics of the Passion are particularly striking. These included fragments of:

- bread from the Last Supper
- the table of the Last Supper (the first Round Table)
- the purple robe of the Passion
- the sepulchre of Christ
- many relics of the Precious Blood
- the Holy Cross
- the Crown of Thorns
- the sponge presented to Jesus on the Cross
- the Holy Lance which pierced his side
- the Holy Shroud which wrapped his body

A remarkable character who links the French and Hungarian monarchies at Senlis in the time of Hugues Capet is Gerbert of Aurillac who, as Sylvester II, was the first French pope, as well as the Pope of the year 1000, the millennium which caused Christendom so many fears and hopes. He first sowed the seeds of a Crusade to liberate the Holy Land, founded the church and the Christian monarchy in Hungary and visited Senlis, encouraging Hugues Capet to form a strong monarchy in France and advising Queen Adelaide to build the chapel to **Saint Frambourg**. He studied occult sciences in Spain, where he was granted wisdom with a kiss by the Queen of the South, and possessed a talking head.

—Troyes—

Map 61, folds 16/17

Troyes, former capital of Champagne and one of the oldest cities in France, is the birthplace of Chrétien de Troyes who introduced the Grail to the world. He was writing in the 1180s and his patrons included Philip of Alsace and Flanders (see **Bruges**), to whom he dedicated his final romance *Le Conte del Graal,* and Marie de Champagne, daughter of Eleanor of Aquitaine, both notable patrons of troubadours.

In 1128 the synod, approving the establishment of the Knights Templar and their rule, written by Saint Bernard of Clairvaux, was held in Troyes, though Hugues, the Count of Champagne, had already joined the order four years earlier. The huge forest of Orient to the east of the city was reputedly the secret world headquarters of the Temple.

In Chrétien's time Troyes was the most important centre of Jewish learning north of the Pyrenees and it has been plausibly suggested that Chrétiens' description of the Grail banquet and procession are taken from the medieval Jewish *seder* ritual and that Chrétien himself was a converted Jew.

Troyes is still famous for its nine churches including ones dedicated to Saint Pantaleon and Saint Mary Magdalen. Apart from one street named after him near the Cathedral the town seems to have forgotten Chrétien.

—Vézelay—

Map 65, fold 15

If Mary Magdalen really landed at Les-Saintes-Maries-de-la-Mer, along with her brother Lazarus, her sister Martha, Joseph of Arimathea and the Holy Grail, then the small town of Vézelay, the major shrine of the Magdalen, clearly merits a visit. During the Saracen invasions of Provence some of her relics were transferred from **Saint-Maximin**—where her fifth-century tomb is still venerated—to the greater security of Vézelay. From then on it became one of the high places of Christendom, a great centre of pilgrimage in itself and one of the four starting-points in France of the way to Santiago de Compostela.

It is these relics in the crypt of the basilica, preserved in a glass cylinder and supported by two angels, which have drawn so many millions of pilgrims to Vézelay throughout the centuries (cf **Sainte Baume** and **Saint-Maximin**).

Despite all depredations it remains the finest Romanesque basilica in France. **Avallon** and its isle, where the Magdalen's brother, Lazarus, who came back from the dead, left his relics, is a mere 15km down the road to the east.

Belgium

*

—Bois-Seigneur-lsaac—

Map 213, fold 18

South of Brussels on the N28, 5km north of Nivelles. Take the road towards
Ophain and in 200yards you will find the Chapelle du Saint Sang ahead on
your left. Ring the bell to the left of thealtar in order to gain access to the chapel
and the sacristy where you can buy postcards, books and medals.

OUR LADY OF THE LIME TREE

The story begins in the eleventh century with a semi-Christianised tree-cult, of
which there are many in Belgium, notably those of Hal, 16km to the north, Foy
and Scherpenheuvel (see Begg, E., *The Cult of the Black Virgin*). The lord of the
region, called Isaac (cf **Fécamp**), planted a wood to the south-east of his castle
and nearby, in the shade of a lime tree, he placed a statue of the Virgin. He
accompanied Godefroy de Bouillon, the grandson of Lohengrin, on the First
Crusade and was taken prisoner by the Saracens. When he prayed to the Virgin
for deliverance she appeared to him and said: 'How can you leave me in the
open air exposed to rain and snow and dare to ask me to help you?' Isaac promised, if he was freed, to build a chapel where the statue of Our Lady would be
sheltered and honoured. This is what happened and the statue was venerated
for two centuries in its sanctuary, when a terrible epidemic struck the inhabitants of Ittre (5km to the west). The statue was carried in procession through
the parish and brought the epidemic to an end, at which, with the authorisa-
tion of the bishop of Cambrai, it was allowed to remain in the village church.

But the Holy Mother of Bois-Seigneur-Isaac did not leave her original children destitute:

THE MIRACLE OF THE HOLY BLOOD

On the Tuesday before Pentecost, in 1405, the lord of the manor, Jean de Huldenberghe or Jean du Bois, was called by his name at midnight by an unknown voice. Before him stood a man of about thirty surrounded by a brilliant light. The figure, opening his cloak, showed the great wounds which covered his body from which flowed streams of blood. 'Look', said he in a plaintive voice, 'how cruelly I have been treated. I pray you, have pity on me, find me a doctor capable of healing me and do me justice.' The knight, who had at first been terrified, was profoundly moved, but could think of no local doctor capable of treating such injuries at that hour of the night. A similar encounter occurred on the following night and on the third evening Jean du Bois asked his brother to keep him company. On this occasion he answered the plea of the stranger with another question: 'Supposing I was able to find this doctor, where could I send him? I know neither who you are nor where you live: Then Christ said to him: 'Take the key of the chapel and go there. You will find me there and you will know who I am.' Jean du Bois did so and saw above the altar Christ on the cross bleeding from many wounds, especially from his open side. Jean's brother was amazed to see him violently agitated and sweating blood all over his body. This was Friday morning and Jean du Bois had experienced his last vision. The priest of Haut-Ittre, whose parish included Bois-Seigneur-Isaac, was woken suddenly from a peaceful sleep by a voice which said: 'Get up, Sir Peter, and go and celebrate the Mass of the Holy Cross in the chapel of Bois-Seigneur-Isaac.'

The priest, though surprised, could only obey and, postponing an anniversary service which was due to take place, he went with his old sacristan to Bois-Seigneur. A group of faithful, including Jean du Bois, who had heard the bell ringing, came in from the neighbourhood. After having unfolded the corporal, Pierre Oste (the name itself is close to the old French word for Host) began the Mass of the Holy Cross. When he came to the Offertory and was about to take the chalice he noticed on the corporal a large piece of consecrated Host which he thought he must have forgotten while he was celebrating on the previous Tuesday. He tried to pick it up but some unseen force prevented him. Suddenly he saw drops of blood issuing from the Host and spreading over the corporal and fainted. Jean du Bois, encouraged by his own experiences, told the priest not to be afraid for this miracle came from God. The blood continued to flow and remained on the corporal for five days to the thickness of one finger and stretching to the length of three fingers. The Host floated on it without dissolving or losing its whiteness. Gradually it coagulated but did not dry completely until after the feast of Corpus Christi. The bishop of Cambrai, Pierre d'Ailly, a well-known figure to whom the pope later entrusted not only his own diocese but the whole of Germany, submitted the corporal to rigorous experiments in baths of wine, milk and soap. He was forced to acknowledge that the bloodstain was not affected in the slightest. He returned the relic to Bois-Seigneur-Isaac and the altar was dedicated to the Holy Blood of the Miracle, the Holy Virgin and Saint John the Baptist on 3 May 1411.

Pope John XXIII, the moderniser of the Catholic church, in a letter of 30 June 1959 (vigil of the Feast of the Holy Blood), recommended to the faithful fervent devotion to the Precious Blood.

The abbey and the chapel are now in the care of the Premonstratensians of Belgium and the procession of the Holy Blood still takes place annually on the second Sunday in September, and the festival of the Holy Blood on 1 July. The confraternity of the Holy Blood established by Cardinal Goossens in 1900 meets here regularly. It is certainly a living a cult.

5km south of Bois-Seigneur-Isaac stands the city of Nivelles, traditionally held to be the home of the Nibelungen.

For further information contact Abbaye des Premontrés, Rue A. De Moor 2, B-1421 Ophain-Bois-Seigneur-Isaac, telephone 0 67/21 24 73.

—Bruges—

(The Basilica of the Holy Blood
Map 213, fold 3)

From the belfry in the market square the chapel is a short walk down Breidel Straat. A town plan, which is essential for exploring Bruges, can be obtained from the Information Office in the same square, the Burg.

At Bruges, one of the most beautiful cities in the world, the Holy Blood and the Holy Grail come together. According to the traditions, Thierry of Alsace, the only successful commander of the Second Crusade, was given by Baldwin III, King of Jerusalem, some of the blood of Christ in token of his gratitude. On his return to Bruges he donated it to the city after a triumphant entry on 7 April 1150, or possibly 3 March 1148. Over eight centuries the annual procession to commemorate this event has been the most famous and sumptuous in the world. It takes place every year on Ascension day at 3pm. Thierry's son, Philip of Alsace was the patron of Chrétien de Troyes who dedicated *Le Conte del Graal* to him. In this book the Grail first enters European literature.

A further important factor in the story concerns the ruling families of Alsace, Burgundy, Habsburg and France, all lords of Bruges and all notable descendants of the Merovingian bloodline and, hypothetically, of Mary Magdalen.

The lower chapel, austere in its Romanesque brickwork, is dominated by an aquiline golden pelican above the altar, feeding its young with the blood from its breast. Both here and in the upper chapel the observant visitor will notice a number of representations which suggest a conscious intent to include the Grail along with the Precious Blood. The upper chapel has suffered much from the vicissitudes of time, war, revolution and the elements, and has been restored in lavish Victorian polychrome. The fifteenth-century windows are now in the Victoria and Albert museum in London. It is in the right-hand chapel, behind a magnificent silver sanctuary, that the relic of the Precious Blood is concealed. It is taken out for veneration and may be kissed by the faithful every Friday in the lower chapel from 8.30am to 10.00am, and in the upper chapel from 10.00am to 11.00am, and 3pm to 4pm. During the Fortnight of the Holy Blood (3-17 May) it is exposed daily. On Ascension Day it forms the focal point of the great procession.

MUSEUM

Before entering the upper chapel you will find to the right a small museum under the care of the noble brotherhood of the Holy Blood. Among many beautiful and interesting objects, the showpiece is the magnificent relic of 1614, made to contain the Holy Blood. The black diamond in the centre of it is said to have belonged to Mary Queen of Scots. Various items recall how the sacred relic was hidden and preserved in times of trouble. It was kept safe during the times of the iconoclastic fury of the Gueux, who occupied the town from 1578 until 1584, when it was recaptured by the Spanish army. The leaden case, in which it was buried by Pérez de Malvenda in his garden during this period, is also on display. Its preservation during the French Revolution owed much to the de Péléchy family. The Baroness, whose portrait is in the museum, walled it up in her house in the Rue Traversière until it was safe to return it to the chapel in 1819. It was Napoleon who preserved the upper chapel from the worst excesses of the revolutionaries, thus making possible its future restoration. During the two world wars when the city was occupied by the Germans the relic was taken for safe keeping to the episcopal residence.

The pelican, believed by the medieval bestiaries to feed its young from the blood of its own breast, was a favourite symbol for Christ, referred to by Thomas Aquinas in his hymn *Adoro Te* as the pious pelican. The feast of Corpus Christi, for which he wrote the Office, was instituted thanks to the visions of Juliana of Liège (cf **Orvieto**). The pelican was also a famous alchemical vessel for distilling spirit by means of circulation.

Spain and Portugal

Spain

*

—Carrea—

Map 441, fold 7C

Of the various Asturian Grail sites none had more magical healing properties than the cauldron of Nuestra Señora del Cebrano in the Templar enclave just north of the Somiedo National Park either side of the O481 from Caranga de Abajo to the river Luna. This famous copper vessel cured both headaches and impotence depending on which portion of the anatomy was lowered into it, accompanied by the appropriate prayers (cf **Carrizosa**). Alas, the Templars were no longer here to protect it and the guardian presence of a Black Virgin was not enough to prevent its theft a few years ago.

—Carrizosa—

Map 444, fold 21P

Halfway between Cludad Real and Albacete, 12km south-east of
Alhambra on the road to Villanueva de los Infantes

Situated between Merlin's Cave of Montesinos at Ruidera (see our *On the Trail of Merlin* pages 193-5) and the Templar castle of Alhambra which guarded the route to it, Carrizosa was, until the Spanish Civil War of 1936-1939, the home of an interesting Grail.

It was preserved in the sanctuary of Nuestra Señora de Carrasca (pine-oak), a Black Virgin that perpetuates an ancient tree-cult. The bronze cauldron, like

65

that of **Carrea** (qv), was an effective healing agency against headaches and barrenness, but only if kissed on a part that had never been kissed before. Alarcón (see Bibliography) was told by a local peasant that it had been stolen and buried by a poor man whose wife taunted him with the fact that their twelve children were fathered not by him but by the cauldron.

—O Cebreiro—

Map 441, fold D8

O Cebreiro is an ancient Celtic village near the mountain pass of Pedrafita (3 638ft). It is associated with both the Holy Blood and the Holy Grail. Nestled against the bare mountainside, the *pallozas*—thatched, low stone cottages—have remained unchanged in style for 1500 years.

The church, with its *hostal*, has been an important staging post between Aurillac and Galicia on the French Road to Santiago de Compostela. The silver reliquary that contains the Holy Blood was given to the church in 1486 by Ferdinand and Isabella, the monarchs, after they stayed here with the monks on a pilgrimage to Compostela. The miracle of O Cebreiro is mentioned as authentic in papal bulls of Innocent VIII and Alexander VI.

Legend has it that in the early fourteenth century on a Sunday of terrible storms a monk from Aurillac was celebrating Mass in the chapel. The only person to turn up for the service was a peasant from Barxamaior. The priest of little faith thought to himself that this man was a fool to take the service so seriously since he felt that what he was doing was mere hocus pocus (cf **Bolsena**). But at the moment of consecration he was overcome by strange fears and watched in horror as the bread turned into bleeding flesh and the wine thickened, darkened and started smelling of blood. The priest fainted and as the peasant tried to save him he died in his arms. The peasant also died shortly afterwards and both men were buried in the church where the holy blood relics are still preserved in ampullas of glass and silver.

The legend of the Galician Holy Grail, as the chalice came to be called, spread throughout Europe and O Cebreiro became the focus of a local addition to the Grail corpus as follows: nine days before Good Friday, Galahad, 'the hoped-for one', left the court of King Arthur and the Round Table, having refused the King's offer of his sword, his shield, his spurs and the honour of knighthood. He journeyed without rest over hill and vale until he reached the sea. Here he found a ship with the Grail emblazoned on its sail, a red cross at the masthead and a silver star on the bowsprit. The vessel carried him to a rocky coast where a sword from heaven embedded itself in the cliff. As Galahad drew it out, the cleft turned into a rosy path which led him on. A ploughman told him that this fair land, in which he had disembarked, was Galicia. In a dark forest he overcame a fearful dragon and discovered the golden shield destined for him. A beautiful princess then fastened on him golden spurs, brought by a page on a silver tray, but he knew he must not dally with this fair maiden of the sea-green eyes and the flaxen tresses, whose smile promised love. He went on his way and on Good Friday reached the summit of O Cebreiro. All doors opened in front of him until he reached the altar where he knelt and offered up his sword. As he raised his eyes he saw on the communion table the chalice of the Holy Grail, with the fresh red blood, which had been preserved in it for centuries.

You can turn back the centuries by staying in the hostel of O Cebreiro.

—El Escorial—

Map 444, fold 3 and 447, fold 7

The Abbey and Palace of San Lorenzo de El Escorial were built by King Philip II at the height of Spanish imperial power at the central point of the Iberian peninsula in honour of Spain's Grail saint, Lawrence (cf **Huesca**, **Rome** et al) as a mausoleum for his dynasty and the still point from which he could rule the turning worlds. His armies defeated the French at Saint Quentin on Saint Lawrence's day, 10 August 1557, and his father, the Habsburg Emperor Charles V, died a year later. Both events inspired Philip to undertake this vast project, which he personally supervised, and which took 1500 builders twenty-one years to complete. It is the largest and last of the great imperial buildings consciously designed and constructed, if not literally as the Grail Castle (see **Castel-del-Monte** and **Karlstein**), at least as a symbolic world axis, by a member of the Grail family who wished to be both Christian and initiate of the mysteries (but cf **Neuschwanstein**). It is built in the shape of Saint Lawrence's gridiron, and echoes the plan of Solomon's Temple. Solomon and David and their successors are present in the huge statues above the entrance in the Kings' Courtyard. The palace, which was designed to contain in art and books all the knowledge accessible at the time, is orientated towards the old capital **Toledo** and its successor, **Madrid**, as well as to the sunset on the feast of Saint Lawrence, and the occultation of the bright star Spica in the constellation of Virgo on the Feast of the Assumption, 15 August (cf **Jaén**).

A group of sages, architects, geologists, doctors and philosophers, whose names are unknown, selected the site between 1560 and 1561, influenced, perhaps, by the presence of many springs and slag-heaps of worthless stones, rejected like Christ and the Grail, and indicating hidden riches.

If the Grail is here, as depicted in Titian's *Last Supper*, the spear of the Habsburg ancestors is also commemorated in El Greco's *Martyrdom of Saint Maurice and the Theban Legion* in the Chamber of Honour of the New Museum. Philip II preferred Cincinnato's *Martyrdom of Saint Maurice*, to be found in the church in the third chapel on the right as you approach the altar.

Philip wished El Escorial to be the launching-pad for the counter-Reformation and the re-establishment of a Catholic world order, and he assembled relics from all over Christendom—7500 of them, including wood from the True Cross as well as secret knowledge, some from none too Catholic sources, in order to establish a mighty generator of spiritual power.

We made a final visit to El Escorial, several years after our first, after we had written our entry and handed our entire text to the publishers, just to refresh our memories. Our first surprise was that the day of our arrival, 21 May, coincided with the birthday of Philip 11(1527). He would have appreciated this coincidence as the dates for the laying of the first stones of both the church and the monastery were carefully chosen so that the horoscopes of these two events should correlate as closely and as harmoniously as possible with his own. Secondly, we came across a marvellous book by Professor René Taylor, *Arquitectura y Magia, Consideraciones sobre la idea de El Escorial* (Ediciones Siruela, S.A. 1992) in the bookshop named Arias Montana after the esoteric Grail Christian who collected on the King's behalf the great library that contained all the hidden wisdom of writers past and contemporary.

The Grail of El Escorial is the Philosopher's Stone. Its architect, Juan de Herrera, wrote a treatise on the cubic figure, according to the principles of Ramón Llull. Llull is one of the unsung patron saints of twelfth-century Grail Christianity—mystic, magus, astrologer, alchemist and mathematician. Herrera had over one hundred of his works, or those by Llull's followers, in his personal library. He took a special interest in the painting by Cambiasso on the vault over the choir and entrance to the church showing God the Father and God the Son resting their feet on a cubic stone while the dove of the Holy Ghost hovers above them. It mirrors the Coronation of the Virgin above the High Altar.

The library with its remarkable wall and ceiling paintings of the seven liberal arts, culminating with astrology and theology, is the greatest repository of esoteric teaching in Spain. Montano marked each book that was particularly esoteric—and potentially dangerous—with 5=1, indicating his belief that human selfhood is divine.

—Guadalupe—

Map 447, fold 23

We had handed in our text to the publishers and were on a relaxed tour of Extramadura, revisiting favourite places like Guadalupe, whose names mean *hidden river* or *underground stream*, home of the famous Black Virgin who is the Patron of the Province and the Queen of all the Spains. While admiring again the paintings by Zurbarán in the Queen of Spanish sacristies we noticed that one of them celebrated a blood-miracle. Father Pedro de Cabañuelos entered the Order of Saint Jerome here (the same order as at **El Escorial**) at the age of fifteen, and while still young became successively novice master (1432) and prior, renowned for his saintliness.

One Saturday, while saying the Mass of the Virgin, he was tempted by the devil with doubts as to whether the Body and Blood of Christ could really be contained in the Eucharist at the same time. At once a cloud descended over the altar so that he could no longer see the Host or the chalice. He prayed for help and forgiveness from Christ and the Virgin. Little by little, the cloud lifted and the altar became bathed in bright light but the chalice was uncovered and empty and the Host was missing. He started praying again for forgiveness. Then from on high descended the radiating Host, which landed on the edge of the chalice and blood distilled into it until it was full. Divine blood imprinted itself on the chalice. The bloodstained corporal can still be seen in the magnificent reliquary-chamber. The Holy Grail of Guadalupe is, however, the miraculous Black Virgin herself.

—Huesca—

Map 43, fold 3

Huesca is where the Spanish history of the Holy Grail begins. As the Roman city of Osca it was the birthplace of Saint Lawrence. He became a deacon of the Church of Rome whose possessions were in his care. He was a close friend of Pope Sixtus II and was martyred by roasting on a gridiron a few days after the execution of the Pope on 10 August AD 258. Before his death, he entrusted the chalice, used by the Popes for celebrating Mass, to two Spanish legionaries who were returning on leave. They delivered it with a letter to the saint's parents, Orencio and Paciencia, who lived in the suburb of Loret, which received its name long before the present church there of the Holy House of Loreto. The earliest evidence for the dispatch of the cup by Saint Lawrence is to be found in parchment No 136 of the collection of Martin the Humane in the archive of the Crown of Aragon and in a fresco in the church of St-Lawrence-Without-the-Walls in **Rome**.

Is there anything to show that this might be the cup used by Jesus at the Last Supper? The most significant evidence is to be found in the words of the Consecration in the ordinary of the Mass used throughout the Catholic Church. These words, which are based on the usages of the early Church in **Rome**, include the phrase 'taking also *this* excellent chalice into His holy and venerable hands'.

From, at the latest, the period of the establishment of the Visigothic Church in Spain in the fifth century, until the Arab occupation following the battle of Jerez de la Frontera in 711, the Grail was kept in the church of San Pedro el Viejo. *(See Plate 26)* The fact that almost all the churches in Aragon connected with the Grail, except for **San Juan de la Peña**, are dedicated to Saint Peter has been interpreted in two diametrically-opposed ways: either there is a shift which led to some dubious earlier dedication being covered up by a new adherence to the guarantor of orthodoxy, or the presence of the true cup of the Last Supper led to identification with the first Pope, who had been a participant and probably used the Grail to celebrate Mass in **Rome**.

San Pedro el Viejo has a remarkable Romanesque cloister whose capitals and sculptures give a number of clues to the one-time presence of the Grail. One capital shows the Last Supper and another a cup-shaped font as baptismal vessel of transformation. Two others show the Temptation in the Garden, where a strange angel passes a cup to Jesus, and the breaking of bread at Emmaus.

The tympanum over the doorway between the church and the cloister shows the Epiphany, with the three Magi making their offerings in separate Grail-like containers.

More curiously, Alfonso I, El Batallador, who came to the throne in 1104 and is buried with his monkish brother, Ramiro II, in the chapel of Saint Bartholomew, assumed many of the attributes of a messianic leader of a Holy War or of a Grail-King, to the extent that some troubadours called him Anfortius, a name close to Wolfram's Amfortas. It was he who introduced the Templars into Aragon and he entered the order himself in 1130. In his will he

left to the Temple his horse, his sword, his armour and a third of his kingdom
(cf **San Juan de la Peña**).

—Jaca—

Map 443, fold 28E

Jaca played a prominent part in the resistance to the Moorish invasions from
the eighth century. In 1035 it became the capital of the new kingdom of Aragon,
as well as the seat of its bishops. The cathedral, one of the oldest in Spain, was
built to house the Holy Grail.

Between its stay in **Sásabe** (qv) and its installation at Jaca, the Grail spent
some thirty years between 1014 and 1045 in Bailo, 12km west of **San Juan de
la Peña**, where the king, bishop and court had taken up their residence. His
son, King Ramiro I of Aragon, rebuilt Jaca and established his court here. In
1063 the Cathedral was completed and in 1071, the papal legate, Cardinal Hugo
Candido, visited Aragon with the mission of establishing the Roman Liturgy
here in place of the Visigothic one then in use. He stayed at **San Juan de la Peña**
and was particularly anxious to celebrate the first mass in the Roman rite in
the kingdom of Aragon with the venerable papal chalice of the Last Supper. So,
with the agreement of the bishop of Jaca, the Holy Grail was transferred to **San
Juan de la Peña** for this purpose. It was never returned despite lengthy recrimi-
nations by the bishop and chapter of Jaca.

—Jaén—

Map 446, fold 20

The main argument for including Jaén is that it, rather than **Toledo**, was the
place where the Visigothic Kings had hidden the table of Solomon (see *Atienza's
Guía de la España Griálca*). For this reason the Moorish commander, Tarik, sent
his armies northwards to **Toledo**, on a detour to capture the area of Jaén. The
present city owes its name to an oracular shrine of the Mother Goddess Aurigi
(she who engenders gold) which the Arabs pronounced *Yayyan* or *Xauen*. A
local gipsy prayer alludes to the table of the Moorish King in connection with
the dragon of the spring of the Magdalen in the district still named after her,
which guarded in its cave a jewelled golden table that had belonged to King

Solomon. The original hiding-place seems to have been a cave in the mountain of Saint Catherine who, along with the Magdalen, personifies divine wisdom comparable to the Shekinah, for which Solomon's Temple was built. She is also represented threefold in the nursing Virgin of the underworld (now in the cathedral), the once-black Virgin de la Capilla, now in the Chapel of Saint Andrew, and the Santo Rostro, the Holy Face of Christ, imprinted on one of the napkins of Saint Veronica (cf **Rocamadour**), exposed in the cathedral each Friday after 11am and 5pm Mass. According to Atienza this is clearly a woman's face with beard and moustache added.

The most striking evidence for the presence of the Grail in Jaén concerns stones fallen from heaven. A wooden panel in the cathedral choir shows two men, a laurel-crowned hero or king with a sword, and a sage, Jewish or Muslim, gazing at a constellation, probably Virgo, with, between them, a large stone sphere that reaches up to their knees. If this is indeed a representation of the Grail as a stone from heaven it seems to be connected with the phenomenon that the brightest star in Virgo, Spica, represents both the fruit of the Virgin's womb and the wheatear of Eleusis. It disappears from the skies of Spain on the Feast of the Assumption (the Dormition or death of the Virgin) on 15 August, and reappears on 8 September, the Feast of her Nativity (cf **El Escorial**). Many other Grail-stones can be seen on the panels, including three being offered by maidens to a Bishop. Another shows Christ in the house of Mary, Martha and Lazarus, with, at his feet, resting on three steps, three full-bellied Grail-jars. *(See Plate 29)*

Just outside Jaén, in the *cerro Contreras*, some stone, head-like spheres, with undecipherable inscriptions, were discovered in 1978 near a labyrinth destroyed by quarrying.

—Llutxent—

Map 445, folds 28 and 18

The Muntanya Santa of Llutxent (Lucente) is situated some 26km east of Xátiva on the C322 Gandia road. Follow the road through the village and take the last turning to the left towards Pinet. The footpath to the hermitage, lined by the Stations of the Cross, is indicated by a cross between the last houses in Llutxent up the hill to your left, while the road to the priory is the first on the left after the cross.

We drove first to the old, half-ruined Dominican priory on the summit, recently used as a drug rehabilitation centre and now undergoing restoration.

Passing the building on your right, take the shaded avenue through a pine-grove to the stone altar and memorial of the miracle of the corporals. Linger a while and enter the little sacred grove behind and enjoy the silence within it.

The story, which had repercussions all along the route from Llutxent to Daroca almost 300 kilometres to the north in Aragon, has a number of features in common with other Holy Blood sites such as **Lucca, Sarzana, Bois-Signeur-Isaac, Bolsena** and **Niedermünster.** A short time before the capture of **Valencia** by King Jaime I of Aragon in 1238, advance guards of the Christian army were patrolling as far south as Llutxent and set up their headquarters on the top of the sacred mountain known as the mountain of the Rock (Daroca). Two of their leaders came from Ayerbe and Luna, towns near **Huesca** and **San Juan de la Peña**, where the Grail had been hidden before finding its final resting-place in **Valencia**.

According to the saga of Llutxent, Mass was being said for the expeditionary force on the rock from which the mountain took its name, and the celebrant had just consecrated six hosts, one for himself and one each for the five captains, when sentries sounded the alarm. A Moorish army had sallied forth from the castle of Xiu, a short distance to the north, and were attacking the mountain. All the Spaniards left Mass for the battle and the priest placed the hosts in altar cloths (corporals) and hid them in a hollow under the rock. When they had beaten off the attack, the captains returned to resume their devotions and give thanks for the victory. The priest took out the coporals and unfolded them to find that the hosts had disappeared, leaving behind them what seemed to be pools of fresh blood. Encouraged by this miracle, the soldiers returned to the attack with the corporals, placed by the priest, Monsignor Mateo Martinez, on a mule, as their talisman. They captured the castle of Xiu and made a great slaughter of the Moors. After a Te Deum of celebration the captains disputed which of them should have the honour of bringing the sacred relics to his native town. Father Martinez solved the matter by placing the corporals in an ark on the back of the mule, leaving it to God to guide the animal to His destination of preference. It wandered north through Pinet, Barxeta, around **Valencia** to Lliria of the white wines, into Segorb, Xerica and Teruel until it finally reached Daroca and dropped dead as it entered the *Puerta Baja*. Father Martinez' solution had brought the relic to his home town where he was the parish priest.

Apart from the altar stone surmounted by a metal cross with the six round red blood stains, the cloister of the Priory should be visited for its well-restored capitals depicting the story of the miracle. Scented pines and herbs surround the sanctuary in an otherwise fairly barren countryside.

The church is open on 24 February, Corpus Christi (Thursday after Trinity Sunday); 4th August (St Dominic); 8th September (Nativity of the Virgin).

The hermitage further down the hill at the top of the Way of the Cross, still attended by its nuns, contains a wonderful series of eighteenth-century *azulejos* (tile paintings) from Manises, depicting with great imagination the history of the miracle of Llutxent.

Llutxent seems always to have been a sacred mountain, a special place. The name in Spanish, Lucente, has much to do with light and enlightenment and many miraculous apparitions of spheres of light have been reported both from Moorish and Christian times.

—Madrid—

Map 444, fold 13 and 447, fold 17

The blood relic of Saint Pantaleon, removed from **San Pantaleón de Losa**, is now housed in the magnificent reliquary gallery, with 4000 other precious relics, in the Convent of the Incarnation (Convento de Ia Encarnación) near the Royal Palace. The blood reliquary of bronze gilt, supported by two angels, can be seen to the right immediately on entering the chamber. The blood, which looks dark and solid, liquefies annually between the evenings of 26 and 27 July, becoming pink and frothy. This is the feast of Saint Pantaleon (see also **Ravello**) when great crowds come to venerate the miraculous occurrence in the church. Our guide (a guided visit of forty minutes is necessary) told us she had witnessed the liquefaction. A Madrid haematologist writes in the introduction for the Guide that he cannot explain the event scientifically, but wonders if Saint Pantaleon, a famous physician, has left us a true scientific challenge. The convent, which was founded in 1611 for the Augustinian nuns, who are still in residence, by Margaret of Austria, Philip Ill's queen, is open to the public on Wednesday and Saturday from I0.30arn-12.30pm and 4-5.30pm, and Sunday from 11am-l.30pm.

—Montserrat—

Map 443, fold 35H

Montserrat is often called the Grail Mountain, and the first distant glimpse of it as you approach it from any part of Catalonia, especially from the north along the A18, will tell you why. It is claimed that here Goethe, writing to von Humboldt, coined his famous last line from Faust: 'The eternal feminine draws us on and up', a Grail description if ever there was one. Wagner is said to have envisaged his *Parsifal* here (but cf **Ravello**), and the Green Michelin Guide states this as a fact, although Wagner's son knew nothing about it. Louis Bouyer, however, a notable scholar, states that it seems almost certain that it was Montserrat which inspired Wolfram's *Munsalwasche,* and that Wagner thought so too.

The only book of folklore available in the bookshop on our last visit was in Italian and tells how Saint Lawrence, before his martyrdom, entrusted the Holy Grail to a disciple who hid it in a rugged mountain. It adds that medieval accounts from England and Germany saw in Montserrat the Munsalwasche of the Holy Grail. A group of ascetical Knights became its guardians and the purity of their lives foiled the plot of the devil to destroy it.

Montserrat is where the feminine principle, alternately lost and found, plays hide-and-seek with us. It was originally a city abandoned to perverse pleasure, which, shaken by a violent earthquake at the time of the Crucifixion, was transformed into the rocky towers and parapets we see today. But, in the grottoes beneath the savage exterior, the laughter of girls can still be heard. Love and laughter were restored when a Temple of Venus was founded here in AD 197. With the coming of Christianity this was destroyed, though the mountain's link to the eternal feminine survived through its Black Virgin, La Moreneta, and through a curious religious order of women who remained there until 976 when Count Borrell of Barcelona replaced them with twelve Benedictines from Ripoll. La Moreneta, carved, according to legend, by Saint Luke, was brought by him or one of the apostles to Barcelona and hidden in a cave at Montserrat during the Moorish invasion.

The Christianity which flourished here belonged to the age-old way of initiation, that of the esoteric Grail tradition. There is a path on the outside mirroring another, within, linking miles of caves. The most distant, perilously-perched hermitages, like Sant Gironi, were reserved for the neophytes, who worked their way back by stages to the central monastery. In one of these cabins, Raymond of Lusignan, who retired here after the departure of his wife, the fairy Mélusine, mother of the Grail lineage, chose to spend his life of penance and recollection.

Buildings come and go, but rocks and mountains endure. Montserrat was searched and destroyed very thoroughly in 1811 by the French who seem to have been looking for something important. Did they find it? Probably not, for the spirit of the place, its topographical uniqueness, its mini-ecostructure and microclimate and its legends are not something you can take back to the

Louvre. Truly this is the house of God, and, to prove it, there is a staircase called, as at Bethel, Jacob's Ladder (see **London**). L.S. Gogan in *Ireland's Holy Grail* (Brown and Nolan, Dublin 1932) writes: 'The Grail of Monserrat at one time attracted an annual pilgrimage of ten thousand people.' He explicitly differentiates it from the **Valencia** chalice.

—Nájera—

Map 442, fold 17

In 1044 King Garcia VII of Navarre was hunting in what is now Nájera. His falcon followed a partridge into a cave at the foot of a cliff whence a mysterious light emanated. The king entered and found there a Black Virgin, surrounded by thorns and, at her feet, a vase of lilies, a bell and a lamp.

Following his great victory of Calahorra, he founded an order of chivalry, dedicated to *La Terraza* (jar), in honour of the Virgin's vessel. Thus a prototypical Grail-cult lies at the origin of Nájera at the foot of the Sierra de La Demanda del Santo Grial. The Virgin, of various names, can still be seen in her deep, dimly-lit grotto around which has been built the magnificent church and Monastery of Santa Maria La Real.

Hugging its purplish, blood-coloured cliffs, Santa Maria La Real is a magnificent example of a harmonious blend of different architectural styles. In complete contrast to the natural simplicity of the Virgin's cave opposite stands the ornate gilt seventeenth-century retable. In a central place of honour above the altar stands *la terraza*, the two-handled glazed jar full of white lilies, on which are depicted the falcon and the partridge—by now firm friends—with the bell and the lamp of the legend. Lucy, the saint of light, who restores sight to the blind—an occasional feature of Grail sites (cf **Arlesheim**) signifying the enlightenment of inner vision—is venerated in a glass-fronted recess to the right of the altarpiece. The capitals and carvings in the cloisters with a multitude of green men, a king holding a head in front of his genitals and a bird pecking off a man's nose, repay close attention.

Ignatius of Loyola, founder of the Company of Jesus, who, like Lancelot and other Grail-knights, laid down his sword to become a saint, lived for four years in Nájera. He accompanied the Duke to the battle of Pamplona in 1521, where he received the wound in the leg that led him to find his true vocation at **Montserrat** two years later. While he was recuperating he asked for some romances of chivalry to read but was given a life of Christ and legends of the saints instead, which deflected him from further knightly adventures to follow the path of sanctity.

—Oviedo—

Map 441, fold 12B

The reconquest of Spain from the Moors began in the ancient kingdom of Asturias. The capital of Asturias is Oviedo and the Cámara Santa, attached to the much later Cathedral, contains the Iberian Ark of the Covenant, the Arca Santa or Ark of the relics. The relics include, among many objects from both the Old and New Testaments, some of the Precious Blood of Christ, a fragment of his Holy Shroud which can still be seen in the Cámara Santa, the Cross of Nicodemus, milk of the Virgin Mary and hairs from the head of the Magdalen. It is thus, both in itself and through its contents, a Grail equivalent. The generally accepted version of its history traces its origin to seventh-century Jerusalem, whence, via Alexandria, Cartagena, Seville and **Toledo**, it found its final refuge from the Moors in Oviedo. According to some accounts the last stage of its journey was overland via Monsacro de Morcin, but strong evidence suggests its arrival at the port of Luarca (100km north-west of Oviedo), having been put to sea in Lisbon. It was guarded by a wolf and in memory of this miracle the name of the port was changed from Subsalas to Luarca, meaning the 'wolf in the ark', though there may also be echoes of the Celtic God Lug.

The original Ark was simply of wood and was placed in Oviedo by Alfonso II 'the Chaste' (791-842), who built the Cámara Santa to house it. In about the year 1030 some priests were rash enough to open the chest from curiosity and were promptly struck blind, like many who had unwisely approached the Ark of the Covenant. In 1075 Alfonso VI, after many days of fasting and penance, opened it again in the presence of Spain's national hero, El Cid. No evil consequences ensued and, in thanksgiving, the King had the chest covered in finely wrought silver. On the lid is a representation of Longinus piercing the side of Christ.

The treasury in the dark apse is kept behind security gates and viewing is only possible with a guide. On view in the cathedral museum is a beautiful, bejewelled portable altar, a twelfth-century diptych featuring, beneath the crucified Christ, a small man climbing out of a cauldron of rebirth.

—Pola de Somiedo—

Map 441, fold 7C

16km west of Carrea as the crow flies

The Grail of Pola de Somiedo was stolen by a woman of the village from a fairy or *xana,* usually associated with water, and was venerated in the church of Santiago de Aquino. Apparently, the fairy lady's attention was distracted while she offered gold to the sun, and the Grail disappeared. She still laments its absence in a song which links it to the Santiago quest.

—San Adrián de Sásabe—

Map 443, fold 28D

We went, following the journey of the Grail, from Siresa to San Adrián de Sásabe, retracing our steps along the HU21O and turned left at Santa Isabel along the HU212 towards Jasa, Aisa and Borau. Just before you reach Borau take a sharp turn to the left (not signposted from the N330) and you will find the beautifully-restored hermitage at the end of this track on the other side of the Rio Lubierre. Sásabe was the final refuge of the Bishops of Aragon during the worst of the Moorish incursions in the eighth century. Here stood the episcopal palace and here, too, the church of Saint Adrian, then dedicated to Saint Peter, which is all that now remains. The Grail was brought here from **Siresa** before the bishops were able to return with it to **Jaca**.

At the time of our visit the church was still being restored and was completely empty.

—San Juan de la Peña—

Map 443, fold 27E

Either approach the monastery from the N240 from where you get a good view of the mountain, or take the minor roads, via Santa María on the C125 from Jaca and HU230, which are more beautiful and interesting.

The Holy Grail of Saint Lawrence and the Last Supper, now venerated in **Valencia** cathedral, was preserved for three centuries in the monastery of San Juan de la Peña. It was removed at the instances of the anti-pope of Peñiscola, Papa Luna, and received by King Martin the Humane in the Chapel Royal of the Aljafería Palace in Zaragoza on Friday 26 September 1399. San Juan de la Peña, a place of refuge for the Christian religion in Aragon during the Moorish occupation, became the pantheon where the kings of Aragon were buried, as well as the starting point from which Don Alfonso the Battler set out for his short-lived reconquest of Spain in 1104. Here he made his proto-Templar knights swear their oath of holy war before the Holy Grail. After his defeat and death at the siege of Fraga he bequeathed his kingdom to the actual Templars. According to popular tradition he awaits the moment of his re-emergence in San Juan de la Peña. *(See Plate 24)*

Here, the handiwork of man and nature blend in perfect harmony. The entrance to the old monastery gapes like the jaws of some mighty petrified fish at the foot of the great cliffs which separate it from the pine-clad meseta where the seventeenth-century 'new' monastery stands.

The legendary foundation of the cult dates back to the eighth century and two brothers, devoted to the hunt, called Voto and Felix. One day Voto, in hot pursuit of a stag, followed it on his horse down the precipice beneath which the monastery now nestles. He had the presence of mind to pray to Saint John for help and his horse landed gently at the foot of the rock. There he was led by the stag to the entrance of a cave hidden by foliage where he found a spring and the body of an ancient hermit lying near it.

The mystery of the monastery is perhaps best savoured in the cloister's capitals. The one called Herod's Castle shows a figure with only his head and feet visible, covering his mouth with his left hand. We have met the figures behind walls and the covering of the mouth before at San Pantaleón de Losa, and Atienza rightly points out that this capital alludes to secret knowledge. Other capitals of particular interest are those of the brothers Cain and Abel, the Last Supper and above all the one depicting Jesus at the great mystery feast of the wedding of Cana pouring forth into large pots the water that he had transformed into wine (cf **Reichenau**).

1. The Abbey of Glastonbury, Grail capital of Britain.

2. ABOVE: Hailes Abbey.
3. INSET: foundations of the major Precious Blood shrine in Britain.

4. Neuvy-Saint-Sépulcre. The Abbé displays the reliquary holding the Precious Blood.

5. Durandal, the sword of Roland, in the cleft rock above the shrine of the Black Virgin in Rocamadour.

6. Window in Bourges Cathedral. Pope
Sixtus II hands the Cup of the Last
Supper to Saint Lawrence.

7. Fécamp. Detail on the tabernacle of the Holy Blood behind the
choir in the Church of the Trinity.

8. Montréal-de-Sos. Our guide dog Emir shows the way to the initiation cave of the Grail Castle.

9. The authors at the Spoulga of Bouan, a fortified cave which was refuge to Cathars and perhaps to the Grail.

10. LEFT: Château d'Usson, last home of the Cathar Grail in France.

11. BELOW: Neuschwanstein, built as the ideal Grail Castle by Ludwig II, d.1886.

12. Linderhof – Blue Grotto, Ludwig II's vision of Lohengrin's Swan Vessel against a background of Tannhauser.

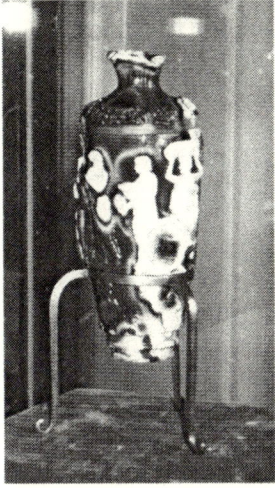

13. The enigmatic and adventurous Onyx Vessel of Brunswick.

14. Reichenau, one of the earliest European shrines of Mary Magdalen. The vessel from Cana of Galilee in which Jesus turned water into wine.

15. Wolframs Eschenbach. Wolfram, poet and knight, author of *Parzival*, honoured in his home town.

16. Externsteine, natural Grail centre of Germany, pinnacle temple for focussing the sun's rays at the winter solstice.

17. Magdeburg Dom. Saint Maurice, commander of the Theban Legion, deprived of the Spear of Destiny.

18. Genoa – Cathedral of San Lorenzo. Lawrence, the Grail martyr, roasted on his grill.

19. Mantua Basilica. Tomb of Longinus – engraving of the centurion who released the Blood of Christ into the Holy Grail with all the symbols of his mission.

20. Mantua Basilica. Altar in the crypt.
The sanctuary can only be opened by eleven separate key-holders.

21. Ravello – Villa Ruffolo. Wagner discovered Klingsor's tower and garden here.

22. Castel del Monte. Frederick II's unfathomable Grail Castle.

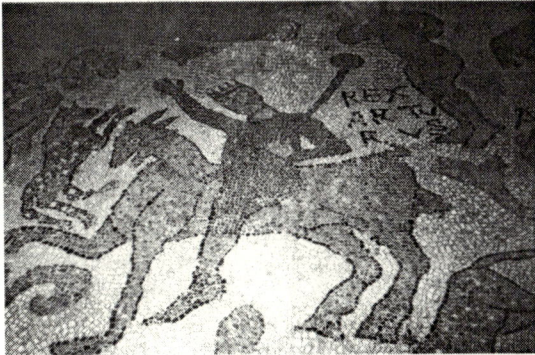

23. LEFT: Otranto Cathedral. Earliest mosaic-representation of King Arthur, 1163–5

24. RIGHT: San Juan de la Peña. Refuge of the Valencia Grail for three centuries.

25. San Pantaleón de Losa. Esoteric Templar chapel of the Mercurial Pantaleón, whose blood liquifies (with the authors).

26. Huesca – San Pedro el Viejo. Home of Saint Lawrence, to which he sent the Holy Grail for safekeeping.

27. Soria – San Saturio, extant example of a Christianised Templar head-cult.

28. Salas de los Infantes. The casket in which the heads of the seven youths and their tutor are venerated.

NOBILIUM CASTELLAE PROCERUM
"LOS SIETE INFANTES DE LARA"
EORUMQUE INSTITUTORIS
DIUTISSIME HIC PIE CONDITA
OCTO CAPITA SERVANTUR

29. Jaén Cathedral. Panel in the choir showing Grail-stone fallen from heaven.

30. Copenhagen National Museum. Gundestrup Cauldron, pre-Christian initiatic vessel.

31. Karlstein. The Emperor Karl IV's Grail Castle in Bohemia, home of the Holy Blood and Spear of Destiny until 1424.

32. Alsace, Saint Nabor. The camel brings the Holy Foreskin to Niedermünster.

—San Pantaleón de Losa—

Map 442, fold 20D

On the BU550, south-west of Bilbao in the direction of Burgos.

Saint Pantaleon is often encountered in Grail sites (cf **Weingarten**, **Ravello** and **Saint Denis**). He was martyred in Nicomedia in 303, shortly before Christianity became the established religion of the Roman Empire. Born of a Christian mother, who died young, and a pagan father, his formative influences were Saints Hermolaus, Hermippus and Hermocrates, an obvious reference to Thrice-Greatest-Hermes, the guide of souls and master of the Emerald Table (see **Toledo**, **Medinaceli** and **Jaén**). Pantaleon had a reputation as a doctor and healer. During one of the many phases of his martyrdom he was, like Saint John (cf **Rome**), boiled in a cauldron and emerged unscathed. When he was finally decapitated, his blood caused a nearby olive tree, to which he was tied, to blossom and bring forth fruit immediately. A phial of his blood, once kept in the church here, was removed to the Convent of the Incarnation in **Madrid** in the seventeenth century. There it reputedly still liquefies annually on his feast day, 27 July.

The origins of the church have been dated back to Bishop Juan de Valpuesta in the ninth century, but its official consecration by the Bishop of Burgos, Don García, was in 1207. According to one authority it was at one time a Templar commandery.

There are many extraordinary rock formations in Spain, but few as striking as the remarkable barbican of San Pantaleón which juts out into the skyline like some great ark about to loose itself from earthly bonds and rocket into the empyrean.

After a minor altercation with a truculent-looking ram and his favourite ewe, amorously ensconced in the west portal, we were able to take stock of this astonishing building. We could discover no traces in the exterior sculptures of any conventional Christian symbolism. To the left of the entrance a half-naked, long-haired Telamon guards the threshold, carrying a sack or fishing-net. To the right there is another strange sculpture: a zig-zag lightning bolt, perhaps, or a petrified serpent. The sculpture of Saint Pantaleon being tortured in the cauldron, on one of the capitals, is still clearly discernible, although it has suffered considerable damage. On the right a better-preserved capital shows three men in a boat. Carved on the arch above the doorway are further curious features in the shape of men entombed in the walls with only their sad and suffering faces and their legs visible, no doubt a representation of the tortured soul entombed in the body. An arch at the rear of the church also shows men thus entombed, but here their faces are calm and serene; perhaps they have now accepted their human fate. Another arch, also at the rear, is constructed like the opening to an initiation chamber with five heads guarding the inner tall, narrow doorway. One of the capitals depicts a man with his mouth wide open, another a grotesque animal face. A further feature on the outer wall, indicating that this was most probably a centre of initiation and the teaching of secret knowledge, is a man's face shown with his mouth gagged and holding up two large hands, turned inwards. One archway is blocked and there are no heads guarding the entrance, but instead there is a man with staring eyes sticking out his tongue. *(See Plate 25)*

—Sant Pere de Rodes—

Map 443, fold 39F

The monastery of Sant Pere de Rodes and the castle of Sant Salvador de Verdera, which stands on the peak above it, are the most romantic ruins on the most dramatic site of the whole Costa Brava. Long before the arrival of Christian hermits and the monks of Saint Benedict this was a great temple to the Pyrenean Venus (cf **Montserrat**), one of whose avatars, Pyrene, was the tragic lover of Hercules. Her stalagmitic tomb is still to be found in the cave of **Lombrives** (qv) where the Grail is said to have rested. An ampulla, containing the Holy Blood, came, according to tradition, to Sant Pere de Rodes along with the head and arm of Saint Peter. According to a parchment found here, copied by the historian Jeroni Pujades in 1600, Pope Boniface IV (608-615), threatened by an invasion of **Rome** by the admiral of Babylon and the armies of Persia, entrusted the most precious relics of the Roman Church to three priests: Felix, Poncio and Epicino. They sailed down the Tiber to the sea and followed the *route of the Gauls* until they reached El Port de la Selva just below the present monastery. They found a cave by a freshwater spring on the mountain and hid the holy relics there. When they returned after some weeks the mouth of the cave was overgrown with thorns and bushes so that they were unable to retrieve the relics. Later, according to the official guide of the monastery, it seems that the head and arm of Saint Peter were returned to **Rome** while the other relics were left to the monastery which was built on the site.

Much of this seems wildly unhistorical, but it is noteworthy that Pope Boniface IV converted the Pantheon, the greatest remaining pagan temple in Rome at his period, from its dedication to the seven principal pagan gods to that of Saint Mary of the Martyrs. Sant Pere de Rodes was a similar conversion. Pagan Corinthian capitals, one of which shows a siren or Morgana with twin tails, testify to a continuity with the pagan past. As so often when such a major transition takes place, Saint Michael, the vanquisher of Lucifer, is present in the name of a tower and chapel.

Of the relics no trace now remains, but Sant Pere de Rodes is well worth a visit both for its associations and the wonder of its site. Once the hillsides were clothed in thick forest; then terraced vineyards took their place. With the departure of the monks whose irregularity of life seems to have perpetuated much of the cult of Venus, and the arrival of phylloxera, the slopes became desolate, and now provide a home only for the fragrant herbs of the maquis with their many shades of green.

—San Vicente de la Sonsierra/— Nuestra Señora de la Piscina

Map 442, fold 17

8km east of Haro

A chronicle relates that Ramiro Sanchez, the Infante of Navarre and grandson of King García VII who founded a Grail-order in **Nájera**, accompanied Godefroy de Bouillon on the First Crusade. Ramiro Sanchez left a will ordering the construction in the Rioja of an abbey church on the plan of the sacred site, the healing Pool of Bethesda, which was the scene of his great exploits in the Holy City. In Jerusalem itself this, the traditional birthplace of the Blessed Virgin Mary, became the church of Saint Anne. Back in La Rioja, Don Pedro Virila de Cardena, the Benedictine abbot to whom Ramiro Sanchez entrusted the erection of the church of our Lady of the Pool and the foundation that was to maintain this cult, set operations in motion in 1136. He chose the site carefully. The well and double basin carved out of the rock were already familiar to us from the pre-Christian baptismal sites we had visited in Brittany. The Celtic hill-fort on the eminence above the church reinforced the impression that this is an ancient place of rebirth. The many tombs of indeterminate date, hollowed out of the living rock around the pools, were further evidence that this was a good place to die in the hope of resurrection. The spring has now dried up—possibly taken to water the surrounding vineyards.

We were immediately struck by the huge coat of arms over the doorway with a preponderance of Fleurs de Lys—the flower of light—symbols of the Merovingian bloodline, and Templar Croix Pattées. In the interior there are the remains of murals showing the plan of the pool of Bethesda and banners bearing the emblem of the *jarra* or *terraza* (see Nájera).

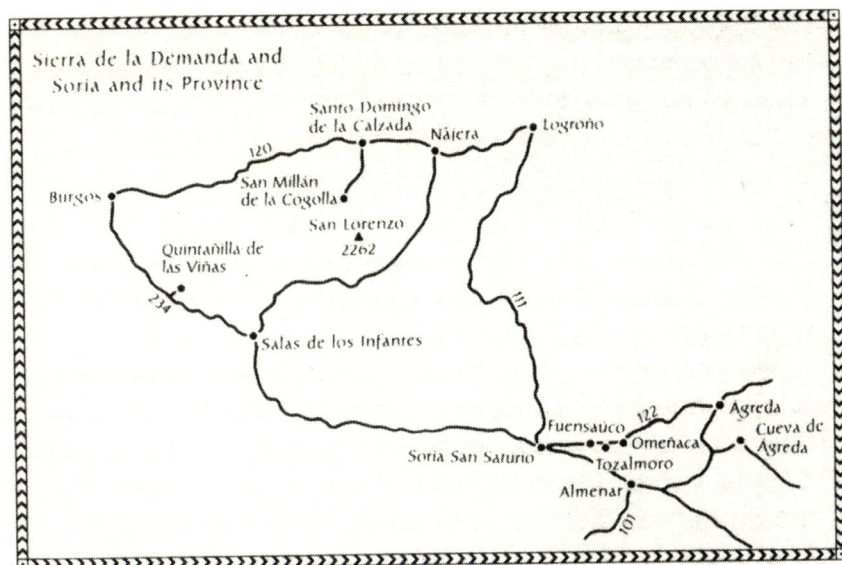

Sierra de la Demanda and Soria and its Province

—La Sierra de la Demanda—
del Santo Grial

The enigmatically-named Sierra de la Demanda (Mountains of the Question of the Holy Grail) is a wild wasteland region bounded by the roads which link Burgos, Soria and Logroño. It is the home of a legend from a thirteenth-century chronicle, Siete Infantes de Lara, which offers striking parallels to the story of Lohengrin, the last Grail Knight. The saga itself, though of great interest, is too long and complex to tell in full, so we shall confine ourselves to those aspects that link it to the mainstream of European Grail literature.

The seven Infantes (royal children) have much in common with fairy-tales of the swan children, but they also have names in a historical context and, above all, relics. Their heads are venerated at **Salas de los Infantes** and their bodies at **San Millán de la Cogolla**.

Each Infante exhibits to perfection one specific virtue—intellectual, amorous, martial, etc, corresponding to the seven planets of traditional astrology. They are brought up by a wise Merlin-like hermit, Nuño Salido, who gives each of them a golden crown to enable them to acquire wisdom, and a white horse to guide them through life. Through family treachery they are killed along with their tutor near Almenar de Soria. Their father, imprisoned in Córdoba, has a son, Mudarra, by the sister of Almanzor, the governor of the city. Allowed to go home to Castille, he leaves her half a gold ring, telling her to give it to Mudarra when he is old enough to join him. When Mudarra reveals himself through the half-ring he is baptized and reborn from under the skirts of the Infantes' mother. He avenges his half-brothers between Salas and Barbadillo and founds a dynasty combining the purest blood of Islam and Christendom. In this he bears some resemblance to Parzival's half-caste brother Feirefiz. He is so like the youngest of the Infantes that he is considered to be his reincarnation.

In one version of the story the Infantes' grandmother takes their golden collars to melt down and transform into a Grail. This corresponds exactly to the oldest literary source of the swan-children written by Jean de Haute-Seille *c.* 1190. In most versions there is one brother whose gold chain is damaged by the goldsmith and is therefore prevented from resuming fully his human form. Thus the story becomes linked to that of Lohengrin, son of Parzival, grandfather of Godefroy de Bouillon and the last Knight known to have seen the Holy Grail.

In an ancient version of the legend Lohengrin is one of seven brothers transformed into swans to escape the murderous intentions of their wicked grandmother. Lohengrin, once he is old enough, wanders the world to right wrongs with his only brother who was unable to resume his human form. It is this swan-brother who draws Lohengrin's boat to Nijmegen (or Antwerp) where he comes to the rescue of the Duchess of Brabant at the Feast of Pentecost. They have many children. One grandchild was Godefroy de Bouillon whose brother, Baldwin, was the first Christian king of Jerusalem. When the Lady of Brabant asks Lohengrin his name, thus breaking an interdict, he returns to the Grail Castle whence he came.

QUINTANILLAS DE LAS VIÑAS *(Map 442. fold 19F)*

To visit the hermitage of Santa Maria of the Vines or of Lara—preferably not like us through three kilometres of fresh hot tar—you must find Don Jesús

Vicario Moreno, its guardian and co-author of the guidebook to it (then in his eighty-fourth year), at the Turismo in the middle of the hamlet. He accompanied us to the church and showed us round.

One glance at the symbolism of the hermitage, within and without, suffices to show that here you are in the presence of alternative Visigothic Christianity. The sun and the moon, with angelic supporters, later rationalised as Christ and his church, are overtly cult-objects either side of the triumphal arch. The sophistication and intricacy of the carvings on the outer walls are impressive. They include oriental animals, not known in seventh-century Spain when the hermitage was built (cf **Rosslyn**): peacocks, guineafowl, pheasants, as well as a lion with a crown on his head, and a profusion of stars, geometrical designs, masonic symbols, grapes, leaves and tree-of-life images. The richness of this decorative art quite clearly speaks of the cult of nature, so characteristic of Celtic Christianity.

From time immemorial Lara, whose seven children can be visited at **Salas** and **San Millán de la Cogolla**, has also been the name of the area, the tower and perhaps, a tutelary mother deity, for Lara was the name of the mother of the seven Lares, the household gods who are the spirits of the ancestors. She was originally an Aquarian goddess who drew gods and heroes from the waters of life. The castle still stood much in its original shape until 1910 when it was cannibalised for building material by local people. The last remaining ruined tower stands out today as a romantic memory on the skyline.

SALAS DE LOS INFANTES *(Map 442, fold 20F)*

Nowhere is the interpenetration of myth and history—a common phenomenon in the Celtic world and in the legends of the Grail—more evident than in Salas. The story of the Infantes of Salas or of Lara (outlined in the introduction to the Sierra de la Demanda) is the pure stuff of fairy-tales. Yet here in the church, above an altar in a chest, venerated annually, are eight skulls, reputedly belonging to the Infantes of Lara and their mentor (cf **San Millán de la Cogolla**). They were never canonised or beatified, and seem to have been far from saintly, while their killing, in a family vendetta, hardly ranks as martyrdom. A further confirmation of their authenticity is to be found in the ruined castle of Lara, just down the road above **Quintanilla de las Vinas** (qv). *(See Plate 28)*

Usually in Spanish towns the main churches are open or, if not, someone nearby has the key. Not in Salas de los Infantes, where the only keys belong to the mayor—difficult to find—and the parish priest—very busy. If you cannot get into the church of Santa Maria, which dominates the town from its hill, have a look at the megalithic tombs and stones at the foot of the long staircase leading up to the church, which is worth a visit, if only from the outside.

On the exterior are numerous representations of Grail and solar motifs. Particularly notable are thirteen heads, carved over the main portico. Having eventually gained entry to the church, we went at once to see the chest where the eight heads are preserved. This is in the choir behind a grille to the left of the high altar. The priest kindly opened the grille for us so that we could examine the chest which contains another, the original one, within it, now much dilapidated. We were also able to read the Latin inscription below confirming that here are indeed the heads of the Infantes and their tutor.

SAN MILLÁN DE LA COGOLLA—MONASTERIO DE SUSO—

(Map 442, folds 21E/F)

Take the LO 834, the first road on the right, 6km south of **Nájera**, to Cardenas, Badarán and Berceo (12km) and follow signs to Monasterio de Suso up the pine-clad hill to the right before you get into the village. For the return journey you could take the beautiful, extremely narrow road to Bobadillo (12km).

The Monastery is open l0am-2pm and 4-7pm (6pm in winter); closed Mondays and 26 and 27 September.

The Monastery of Suso was founded by San Millán de la Cogolla (of the hood, 473—574). It is one of the jewels of Visigothic Spain, completed in pre-Romanesque and Mozarabic style. As you go through the beautiful portico of the church you enter an atrium with eight sarcophagi, seven aligned along the low wall to the left with eight open arches, and one, larger and more ornate, centrally positioned at the far end. These are the tombs of the seven sons of Lara and their tutor Nuño Salido, whose heads are venerated at **Salas de los Infantes**, at the diagonally opposite, southern exit of the Sierra de la Demanda.

Curiously, Nuño's tomb, the solitary one, dates from the fourth century, much earlier than those of his charges, hinting that, whatever brand of Christianity he represents, it is contemporary with that of the famous Christian druid of Galicia, Priscillian.

San Millán was once co-patron of Spain with Santiago. But, like many another saint of the esoteric Grail tradition, he fell out of favour and would be little known today had not the first poet to write in Spanish, Gonzalo de Berceo (1180-1247?), a monk of San Millán and a native of Millán's own birthplace, sung his life in a beautiful poem rich with the love of nature.

His remarkable tomb merits attention. On it he is depicted in splendid robes surrounded by the angelic helpers who raise the soul to heaven. There is a semi-restored capital in the church revealing interesting symbols, including an inverted five-pointed star—belonging to Lucifer, the light-bearer, whose fall earthed the Grail vision, and curious twisted arches over other star motifs.

SIRESA *(Map 443, fold 27D)*

In answer to the Grail-question posed by the Sierra de la Demanda comes the answering echo, the Valle del Hecho (Valley of the Deed). The monastery of San Pedro de Siresa, originally Benedictine, provided the northernmost refuge of the Holy Grail in the Pyrenean foothills for half of the ninth century.

We arrived expecting a ruin, easy of access, but found restoration in full swing and no entry to the church permitted. Atienza is in no doubt that the Grail was preserved in an inaccessible gallery above the western entrance which is still standing. The village of Hecho, 3km to the south, was the site of a Templar Commandery.

SORIA AND ITS PROVINCE *(Map 442, fold 28)*

Soria lies at the eastern edge of the Sierra de la Demanda del Santo Grial and continues the story of the Siete Infantes de Lara (see Sierra de la Demanda). Their presence—and the cult of the head—is much in evidence. All the sites are to be found in the 50km to the east of Soria city. Soria itself was the home of Rosa, known as divine wisdom, beloved of the Grail Emperor, Henry II of Hohenstaufen (see **Castel del Monte**).

On the very doorstep of Soria on the east-bank of the Duero stands the hermitage of *San Saturio* (cross the bridge and take the first road to the right), where there persists as fine an example as could be found of a Templar, baphomet, head-cult. It was formerly part of the Templar stronghold of San Polo. *(See Plate 27)*

Saturio was a Visigothic noble who lived for thirty-six years a life of penance and heroic virtue in a cave on this site and became the patron saint of Soria. But this wise old hermit, presented as bald and bearded, is also the Christianised form of Saturn, who, according to Wolfram and Albrecht von Scharfenberg, was the god who taught Parzival steadfastness, constancy and self-denial, by which the spirit is augmented at the expense of matter.

At *Fuensaúco*, the first village to the left of the N122, one can see depicted on the exterior of the church a group of eight heads, six of them children, one a teacher and another a holy figure.

Of greater interest is the next village to the right, *Tozalmoro*. If you climb on some rubble and peer over the rear wall of the churchyard, you will be rewarded with a glimpse of a blind arcaded window with eight heads enclosed within the semi-circle of the arch. On the eastern exterior of the church, if you look up, you will see a Sheela-na-gig—rare in this part of Spain—a woman holding open her vulva with her legs over her shoulders, to ward off evil spirits.

Finding *Omeñaca*, the next village to the right, is more difficult than it seems. Coming from Soria the sign-post is on the left side of the road, directing the driver off to the left and then under the road on the other side. The church, which you approach through a farmyard, is beautifully restored. It is said that its seven arches opened up spontaneously when the Infantes (see **Salas**) approached it for their last Mass before their death. Note the seven heads above the door and the particularly fine example of a motif, not uncommon in the region, of a great benign, bearded head with a small, young being with large hands beside it.

Somewhere, just to the south-west of the *Cueva de Agreda* where Cacus stole from Hercules the cattle of Geryon in a plain by the Río Araviana, on the way to Noviercas, the Siete Infantes met their end at the hands of their uncle Ruy Velázquez and his men. His castle in Sorian lands is at Almenar de Soria. He betrayed the Infantes by inviting them to a Moor-hunt, whereas in reality he had prepared their assassination by ambush.

MEDINACELI *(Map 443, fold 22)*

Though not in the Sierra de la Demanda, here we encounter a different and more direct Grail-tradition than that of the Infantes de Lara (see **Salas de los Infantes**). When the Muslims captured **Toledo** in AD 711, its greatest treasure, the table of Solomon, was, according to tradition, either hidden in the cave of Hercules there, or taken to the city of Ocilis, near **Soria**, where it was likewise concealed. When the Arabs arrived there, although they failed to find the treasure, their leader, Tariq, renamed the city Medinah al-Shelim, the city of Solomon, in its honour. At the reconquest the Spaniards rebaptised it Medinaceli, the city of heaven, and so it has remained.

What remains of this once-important city is a beautiful, quiet village whose triple arcaded Roman arch, unique in Spain, and Arab castle and gateway still dominate the *meseta* and the Madrid-Zaragoza motorway. The locals know nothing of Solomon's buried table and thought it might be rather hard work to dig for it. But they were well aware that Almanzor, the conqueror-caliph of Córdoba, whose daughter had a mysterious child by the father of the seven

Infantes (see **Salas de los Infantes**), was buried here on 11 August 1002 after his defeat at the battle of Calatañazor. The exact site of his tomb is unknown but is almost certainly between the Plaza de Almanzor and the Arab Castle. It is at least curious that this great leader, with links to the Grail-family of the Sierra de la Demanda del Santo Grial, should share a resting place with the last-reported earthly dwelling of the Table of Solomon which Almanzor's ancestors had striven so determinedly to make their own.

—Toledo—

Map 444, fold 12 and 447, fold 16

Here, one branch of the Grail legend, that of Wolfram von Eschenbach, begins, and here, just as mysteriously, with the advent of the Moors, another ends. When the Visigoths were expelled from France by the Merovingian King, Clovis, they transferred their capital from Carcassone and Toulouse to Toledo. Among the treasures they took with them were the sacred objects removed by the Emperor Titus from Jerusalem to **Rome** in AD 71, which fell into the hands of Alaric when the eternal city was sacked in its turn in 410. Three hundred years later the last Visigothic monarch of Spain, Rodrigo, entered the secret cave under Toledo, which only the King might enter. On the walls he saw prophetically represented the Arab invasion and found a book in which it was written that the Arab race would conquer these lands. After the fall of Toledo Tarik ben-Siyyad found in the cave, among other treasures, a great round mirror which had been made for King Solomon. Spanish legends say that the table of Solomon on which the Jewish Grail, the Ark of the Covenant, had once stood in the Holy of Holies, was taken to **Medinaceli** (see also **Jaén**). Created for Solomon by djinns (desert spirits), it also had the quality of a mirror or scrying-glass, which revealed secrets and far-off things. It became, like the Grail, the symbolic goal of the quest.

Toledo was one of the major centres of learning in Europe, where Christian, Arab and Jewish scholars congregated—in the twelfth century there were 12,000 Jews in the city. Here Kyot learned the secrets of the Grail from Flegetanis, a baptised pagan astrologer of the race of **Solomon**, and passed them on to Wolfram von Eschenbach. Anderson suggests that Flegetanis derives from *Falak*, the Arabic term for the planetary spheres and *Teni*, the designation of first-century Jewish rabbis of the diaspora. Toledo is still the living sacred centre of Spain, as the See of its Primate, and the Visigothic liturgy with its many variations from the Roman rite is still celebrated in its cathedral. Under its beautiful and historic exterior it is honeycombed with caverns and secret passages, but where the cave of Hercules, legendary founder of the city, lies and where the treasure of the Temple may be hidden is likely to remain a mystery, although it was stated by Juan Moraleday Estebán in his *Tradiciones de Toledo*, published in 1888, to be beneath the ruined church of San Ginés, a curious saint, possibly a djinn, in the centre of the city between the Puerta del Sol and the Cathedral.

One of the oldest cities in Europe, Toledo is believed to have been settled by Phoenicians from Tyre and Sidon and there is a legend that Adoniram, who raised the taxes for Solomon to build the Temple, took refuge here. It is claimed that the Jewish colony in Toledo goes back to 500 BC, so much of Solomon's lore concerning the Temple and its contents could have been preserved here.

As we left the city visited the Tavera Palace where we were introduced to a modern Toledan mage who claimed to possess the Key of Solomon which would enable him to discover any secret thing we sought in the city. Unfortunately his duties in the archives were likely to detain him for most of the day so we reluctantly declined his offer of help. He did, however, draw our attention to the stone on which the Virgin Mary left her footprint during a visitation to Saint Ildefonsus, Bishop of Toledo (d. 667), to present him with a chasuble. The stone is now in the Cathedral and has been much worn away by the hands of pilgrims.

A further Grail-like occurrence was the appearance in the middle of the sixteenth century, to poor people panning for gold, of a large ark with a black crucifix in the Tagus near the Alcántara Bridge. The ark demanded to be taken to the Holy True Cross of Toledo. The Christ of the waters was eventually transferred to the Church of Saint Mary Magdalen.

The whole of Toledo is a hermetic sermon in stone, an alchemical process of individuation, lovingly described by Alejandro Vega Merino in his *Introducción al Toledo Filosofal* (Toledo 1989). He tells of a stone fallen from heaven in the Plaza de la Estrella which once stood on the pillar now surmounted by a cross in the little square by the entrance to the city next to the church of Santiago near the mosque, now dedicated to the Christ of Light. Toledo was the city, more than any other, where Jews, Christians and Muslims lived in harmony through the syncretistic Grail-wisdom that is the esoteric heart of all religions.

Inevitably there were difficulties before the defeat of the Moors and the expulsion of the Jews. One involved the lovely mosque of the Christ of Light when it was a Christian church under the Visigoths. Two Jews pierced with a lance the side of an image of Christ on the cross, from which blood flowed copiously. They stole the crucifix, but the blood trail led to their capture and chastisement. During the Muslim occupation the statue was buried in the church grounds with a lighted candle next to it. When Alfonso VI and El Cid reconquered the city the King's horse knelt as it passed the church and the statue was discovered with the candle still alight. A white stone outside the church marks the spot where the horse knelt.

—Valencia—

Michelin 445, folds 12 and 15

The Holy Grail in Valencia Cathedral is the only one claimed to be authentic by the Roman Catholic Church as the chalice blessed by Jesus at the Last Supper and used by the popes in **Rome** until it was sent for safe-keeping by Saint Lawrence to **Huesca** in AD 258. Since 1399 its movements are perfectly documented. It was brought from Barcelona in 1424 by Alfonso V the Magnanimous to his Palacio de Real in Valencia. His brother, Juan, King of Navarre, transferred the Grail to the Cathedral on 18 March 1437. It has remained there ever since except for two brief periods during the War of Independence against France and in the Spanish Civil War. In 1809 it was transferred to Alicante and after a brief return to Valencia in February 1810 it was taken for safe-keeping to Ibiza and later Palma de Mallorca, returning to Valencia Cathedral in September 1813. During that period the Royal Palace, its original home, was destroyed by the Spaniards to deny its use to the French army. On 21 July 1936 it was rescued just in time from the communists and hidden until 30 March 1939 by Señorita Sabina Suey, first of all in her various houses in the city and then in her country residence of Carlet. On 9 April 1939, Maundy Thursday, the Grail was officially received back in Valencia and episcopal High Mass was celebrated in La Lonja, the magnificent fifteenth-century silk exchange, famous for its erotic sculptures. It was finally restored to the Cathedral on its traditional feast-day, 9 July, in the same year, and since 1943 has been venerated in its present setting.

The Grail itself and its setting are rather disappointing unless one can focus on the extraordinary history of the relic, and the fact that of all the objects in the world, it is the one most likely to have been handled by Jesus Christ. You must venerate it from afar, unable to appreciate fully the rich reddish-brown of the ancient agate cup, reminiscent of coagulated blood, or its pure gold base decorated with 28 pearls, two red gem-stones and two emeralds.

The measurements of the actual cup are as follows: height 5.5cm, diameter 9.5cm, thickness 3mm. With its base it measures 17cm by 14.5cm.

One of the puzzles of the Grail is a short (1.5cm) inscription in crude Arabic on its base. This has been variously translated as 'for him who gives splendour'; 'Glory to Mary'; 'the Merciful One' (a favourite Muslim epithet for Allah); 'the flourishing one' or the name of the palace of Almanzor in Córdoba (see **Medinaceli.**)

Directly leading off the chapel of the Holy Grail is the Cathedral museum which includes two paintings of the Valencia school by Juan de Juanes, of Christ. One shows him in front of the Valencia Grail which is filled with a dark red liquid and the other shows Christ at the Last Supper with Saint John lying in his arms and the Grail before them on the table.

—Yebra—

Map 443, fold 29E

In 712, the year after the Muslim invasion of Spain, Acisclo, the bishop of **Huesca**, and his clergy, fled the city with their most precious relics, above all the Holy Grail and the foot of Saint Lawrence, to seek refuge in the cave of Yebra in the remote foothills of the Pyrenees.

The story of the Grail in Yebra becomes interestingly confused with that of Saint Orosia. According to one version she is a princess of Egypt whence so many sacred relics (see **Oviedo**) embarked for Spain. She also came via Bohemia, with hindsight an intriguing conjunction, given the identification of the gypsies and their Tarot, steeped in Gnostic wisdom, with both Bohemia and Egypt. Another story makes her a princess of Aquitaine, come to Aragon in search of a husband. But she was also the niece of Bishop Acisclo and so of Aragonese stock herself. The Saracens, under Aben Lupo, eventually arrived. He wished to marry Orosia and on her rejection had her dismembered in front of her uncle, the Bishop, and her brother, Cornelius, who were also martyred. The Grail, fortunately, had already been dispatched for safekeeping to **Siresa**. But its memory lingered on along with the foot of Saint Lawrence.

Little by little Saint Orosia assimilated in her cult many of the qualities of the Grail itself. She was, to begin with, by her very name, the golden one, and her head, now kept in the village church of Saint Martin, is gilded, with a round opening at the top.

After an acerbic dispute, her body was transferred to Jaca where, until recently, it cured demoniacs and hysterical women who were brought there from all over Aragon and southern France. On her feast-day, 25 July, when the

Jaca ceremonies also took place, a pilgrimage is made annually from the church of Saint Martin 10km up to the original hiding-place in the grotto.

The village church is only open for Mass on Sundays. So, as is our custom on occasions like this, we made straight for the simple local pub and ordered coffee and brandy. We were lucky. The owner had a particular interest in Saint Orosia and large pictures of her and her cave were hanging on the walls. He was also in possession of up-to-date literature about the saint and willingly shared it with us. The book that was especially useful to us was *Las Romerías de Santa Orosia.*

Saint Orosia's chapel is only open on the 25 July when the relics are taken there in procession. To find the chapel, turn left before you enter the village from the west and then take the left fork until you come to a road-sign indicating the four hour uphill excursion on foot to the left. If you want to take the very bumpy, serpentine car-route drive straight on and follow the path round.

Portugal

*

—Tomar—

Map 37, fold 15

To experience a Templar round church on the grand scale, still standing in its pristine and mysterious splendour as though for the performance of secret rituals, you must visit the Convent of Christ in Tomar. It was founded in 1160 by Gualdim Pais, Grand Master of the Knights Templar. The Rotunda (see **Charroux** and **Neuvy Saint Sepulcre**) was built on the model of the Holy Sepulchre in Jerusalem, with eight pillars supporting a two-storey octagonal structure crowned with a dome.

Portugal was the most important country of refuge for the Templars after their suppression and they continued to flourish there as the Order of Christ, founded in 1320, whose headquarters was Tomar. Building continued here until the seventeenth century.

Italy

Italy

*

—Bocca di Magra—

Map 428, fold 36, 111

Here, in what is now a pleasant yachting resort with spectacular views to the Apuan Alps across the Magra estuary, is where, in the Roman harbour, at the far end of the village, the Holy Face of **Lucca** and the Precious Blood of **Sarzana** came to rest after their miraculous voyage in 742. Furthermore, the Carmelite Fathers claim that in their monastery chapel of Santa Croce the true Holy Face resides rather than at **Lucca** (q.v.) It is huge, like its more famous twin, with a wonderfully compassionate expression, moving in its simplicity. It was recently examined and restored by the Belle Arte in **Genoa** and found to contain two hollows for reliquaries, of exactly the right size to contain the phials of blood, and in what was traditionally the exact place: just below the nape of the neck. The monks believe that this supports their claim that it is they who possess the original Volto Santo.

—Bolsena—

Map 430, folds 0/17

In 1263 a priest, known only as Peter of Prague, was saying Mass at the tomb of Saint Christina in the church dedicated to her. There were many at the time, both in Bohemia and central Italy, who had doubts about the doctrine of Transubstantiation and Peter was one such doubter. While he held the host over the chalice at the moment of consecration it turned into real flesh streaming with blood. Some drops landed on the stones below the altar and others, falling on the corporal, each took the form of the Holy Face of **Lucca**. Similar miracles at places as far apart as **O Cebreiro, Bois-Seigneur-Isaac** and **Llutxent**, were local wonders, far from the major seat of authority of the Catholic Church. Bolsena is a mere 19km from **Orvieto** with its palace of the Popes where Urban IV was in residence at the time of the miracle. This divine intervention encouraged him to establish the Feast of Corpus Christi.

History relates nothing further about the mysterious Peter of Prague— where he was coming from or going to and why he had a particular devotion to Saint Christina. About the saint, however, there is a considerable evidence linking her to an Ark/Grail-cult. Apart from the gory details of her martyrdom, similar to those of many another early fourth-century Christian maiden, the following legendary accounts are relevant to us. She floated on the stone which still supports her altar and bears her delicate footprints. She came originally from Tyre where Simon Magus, father of all heresies, discovered divine wisdom in the form of Helen whom he rescued from a brothel. From Tyre too came the builder of Solomon's temple in which the Ark of the Covenant and the Shekinah would dwell, as well as the materials from which it was made. Hiram of Tyre later became a central figure in Freemasonry.

At Lloret de Mar on the Costa Brava in Spain, the feast of Saint Christina is celebrated with a remarkable dance in which women break four crystal vessels and pour their sacred perfumed contents on to the ground. The saint's feast, 24 July, is also the vespers of Saint James (Santiago), whose image is carried in procession with hers. The dance is repeated on 26 July (feast of Saint Ann), leaving space for the Spanish national holiday of Santiago in between. July 22 is the day sacred to the Christian Grail-bearer herself, the holy wisdom called Saint Mary Magdalen, who poured precious balm on the feet of Christ. At this time of year the pagan feast of Neptunalia also took place.

A second Saint Christina (d. 330) was born in the area of Mount Ararat, where the Ark of Noah came to rest, called Iberia, and, spared martyrdom, became the apostle of Georgia. An Ark carrying Santiago's body landed at Noya (Noah) (see our *On the Trail of Merlin)* on the Galician coast.

The church of Saint Christina is in the lower town of Bolsena. To reach the chapel of the miracle go through a doorway on the left at the end of the Basilica where the bloodstained paving stone is displayed above the altar. The beautiful altar of the miracle is adjacent, to the left, next to the catacomb which contains the relics of Saint Christina. A remarkable procession in which the streets of the town are paved with floral patterns and representations of the miracle and the Eucharist, takes place annually on the Feast of Corpus Christi.

—Calcata—

Map 430, P19

This is the only site in Italy claiming to possess the true Holy Foreskin of the Infant Jesus. Unfortunately, politically-correct ecclesiastical pressure, connived at by the local priest, forced its withdrawal from circulation some six years prior to our visit in 1992. The Church, it appears, no longer approves of wonder-working relics, especially of such an intimate physical nature. So, along with a host of so-called dubious saints, they have been relegated to the dustbin of pseudo-history. No trace of the relic's passage remains in the church of Calcata Vecchia and no postcards or booklets are available. Calcata, nevertheless, is worth the journey as it is one of the most remarkable small hill towns in Latium, though you will find it in neither the Blue nor the Green Guide. It stands high above the valley of the Teja on a pumice hill, honey-combed with caves.

It was to one of these that a soldier brought the relic which he had looted from Saint John Lateran during the sack of Rome in 1527. Before long the cave became noted for miraculous happenings and the relic was taken to the baronial castle. Thanks to the intervention of a seven-year old girl, Claricia Anguillara, and a wonderful odour of sanctity which filled the Baron's hall, it was transferred to the parish church. There it was celebrated with great pomp every 1 January, the feast of the Circumcision. One of the notable phenomena associated with it was that it appeared in rosy pomegranate tints to anyone who was in a state of grace, while to those in sin it was dark and grey. It was venerated in a reliquary of gold glass enamel and precious stones, about 45cm high and supported by two angels, like its fellow at **Charroux**. Indeed, some traditions hold that it is the same relic, from Jerusalem, taken to **Aachen** by Charlemagne, that was transferred to Charroux and thence to the Sancta Sanctorum of Saint John Lateran, in **Rome**. What purports to be the reliquary is in the Vatican Museum.

The relic continued to produce miracles until quite recently. The brother of one lady we spoke to, who had served with the Italian army in Ethiopia and been captured by the British, had been preserved from almost certain death when he prayed to the Holy Prepuce. The mother of another woman had been healed from a serious illness by its power. All the people we spoke to were desolated by the loss of the relic. Some say it has been stolen; some that it is still in the priest's house at Calcata Nuova; others, more cynical, that the priest sold it. Whatever the case, it has disappeared and is unlikely to be seen in Calcata again.

—Castel del Monte—

Map 431, fold D30

Castel del Monte is surely one of the most enigmatic buildings ever to have been raised in the West. On the site of a former church and monastery, dedicated to the Virgin Mary, it stands on a conical hill, commanding the plain of Bari, but it was not designed like any other fortress. The Emperor Frederick II of Hohenstaufen (1194—1250), *Stupor Mundi,* was the most remarkable monarch of his age and just as mysterious as his castle. He ordered the commencement of the building on 29 May 1240, but it took many years to complete, and although Frederick most likely had intended to live here himself, he never did. It was used from time to time for royal weddings and other festivities and was converted into a prison for Frederick's children by the House of Anjou after the fall of the House of Hohenstaufen in 1266. *(See Plate 22)*

Castel del Monte is a massive octagonal structure almost 80m in height. At each of the eight corners stands an octagonan tower with an internal spiral staircase which leads from left to right. There are eight halls on the ground floor and eight on the upper. They are all of the same size and trapezium-shaped. There is a falcon-loft and a large roof terrace, thought to have served as an observatory. None of the walls of the inner courtyard are the same and according to tradition an octagonal monolithic marble basin once stood here, preserving the Blood of Christ. The positioning of the variously-sized windows is often asymmetrical. There is only one entrance, which leads to the room of the guardian, through which all visitors need to pass to gain access to the interior.

Historians have never been able to reach an agreement about the function of the building. Indeed, without deeper study of the relationship of the angles, positions and shapes of its various structures, it could easily be assumed to be just a folly or bizarre puzzle. However, a detailed examination reveals the castle to be built according to precise astronomical and mathematical laws correlating with the precession of the equinoxes. On the days of the vernal and autumnal equinoxes (21 March and 23 September) the first ray of the rising sun passes through the window above the portal, then through the inner hall and the inner window into the court yard until it falls on a niche in the opposite wall. Inside is a relief of a woman, wearing a Greek garment, who is receiving homage from admirers, which recalls the ancient fertility rites. A further example of sacred geometry is to be found in the fact that if one draws an imaginary line between the points on the horizon where the sun rises and sets at the summer and winter solstices one obtains a perfect rectangle, the centre point of which coincides with that of the castle's in the large inner courtyard that is open to the heavens. This is only possible on the degree of latitude of Castel del Monte. The portal is based on a circumference whose radius is 5.5m, the unit of measure according to which Solomon built his Temple of Jerusalem. Space does not permit to elaborate further on the intricate sacred geometry in evidence here, nor on the building's harmonious relationship to the heavenly bodies. Suffice it to say that Castel del Monte is a document in stone of astronomical, geometric and mathematical correlations, clearly designed as a navel of the world, like Jerusalem, Mecca and Taq-di-Taqdis y in Iran, a Grail in itself to receive the light of the world.

Another castle built on esoteric lines, **Montségur**, has connections to Castel del Monte. Shortly before the fall of **Montségur** in 1244 the son of the famous troubadour Peire Vidal crossed the enemy lines to bring a message of hope to the besieged from the Count of Toulouse: 'Hold on for another seven days. The Emperor Frederick II is coming to the rescue'. Frederick, who was not above persecuting Cathars himself when advantage dictated, did not come, and the citadel fell. But the last of the Hohenstaufen Emperors was, in spite of all his faults, a man of the new age who favoured the ideas of Joachim of Flora. Joachim proclaimed the coming of the era of love and the Holy Spirit as well as seeking to reform the Church to its primitive simplicity.

The castle is open 1 April to 30 September 8.30am-7pm (Feast Days 9am-lpm); 1 October to 31 March 8.30am-2pm (Feast Days 9am-lpm).

—Genoa—

Maps 428 18 and 988, fold 13

SAN LORENZO IN VIA SAN LORENZO

Museum open on Tuesday, Thursday and Saturday from 9.30-11.45am and 3.00—5.45pm. Stop press! On our second visit on 28th September 1993 we found the Treasury had been closed by order of the City Fathers last December and there was no prospect of its re-opening. The woman sacristan agreed that if the ways of God were mysterious, the ways of the Commune were even more so. If you plan a visit check with the Tourist Office before subjecting yourself to the ordeal of Genoese traffic.

The twelfth-century chronicler William of Tyre reported that the *Sacro Catino* or Holy Cup fell into the hands of Genoese crusaders in Jerusalem after the capture of Caesarea. It was said to have been not only the cup of the Last Supper, but also the gift of the Queen of Sheba to King Solomon, carved from one vast emerald. It was brought back in triumph to Genoa in 1102 and installed in the church of Saint Lawrence, the same deacon of Rome who sent the Valencia Grail for safe-keeping to **Huesca** in the third century, and whose relics are in the museum. *(See Plate 18)*

Another legend says that it once reposed in the Temple of Herakles-Melkart in Tyre. This has important associations. It was from Tyre that Solomon brought Hiram to construct the Temple as the permanent home of the Ark of the Covenant. If the Baal (Lord of Tyre) was Melkart, the Lady was Astarte/Asherah/Ashtoreth/Ashtart, the Syrian Goddess of Tyre, Sidon and Byblos, in whose honour Solomon also installed a place of worship in Jerusalem. She is the Queen of Heaven who gives birth to the divine solar child each year on 25 December.

According to Spanish writers the *Sacro Catino* was part of the booty of Almería, conquered from the Moors with the help of the Genoese in 1147, and given to them by a grateful Alfonso VIII of Castille. Sant'Antonio, the Bishop of Florence, claimed it was captured by the Genoese at Tortosa at its reconquest in 1148. The Blue Guide to Northern Italy refers to it simply as 'a 1C Roman glass dish said to have been used at the Last Supper'. It was certainly treated with the greatest honour in Genoa—twelve knights were appointed to guard it and anyone who dared to touch it risked death.

Historically it is known to have been in Genoa since the twelfth century, until Napoleon, a collector of sacred objects, like many dictators, had it taken to Paris, where it was scientifically examined—and also broken. It was returned in 1816 in ten pieces with one missing, which was retained by the Louvre. Its decline from cult object to curiosity seems to date from this period, though Coincy-Saint Palais relates another story according to which the French savant, La Condamine (1701-1774), or, according to another account, the Swiss scientist Bernoulli, had already scratched it with a diamond, revealing it was ordinary glass.

Today it stands in the fine museum of 1956, in the first of the tholoi, or Mycenean beehive-shaped tombs, which are the inspiration for the building. It is hexagonal, like the crystals which are the basic structure of life, shallow, dark-green, with a golden rim, mounted on a wrought-iron tripod, like a tiny television dish or radio-telescope for watching the heavens and receiving any messages that might be coming through the ether. It bears its scars nobly, and is a fine object for contemplation. Other relics in the museum include the ashes and head of John the Baptist.

—Lucca—

Maps 428 K13 and 988 fold 14

The *Volto Santo,* or Holy Face of Lucca, honoured in Saint Martin's Cathedral, was the handiwork of Nicodemus. He was 'a ruler of the Jews', a Pharisee, who came to Jesus by night and asked how it is possible to be born again when one is old. Jesus answered: 'Verily, verily I say unto thee, except a man be born of water and the spirit, he cannot enter the Kingdom of God ... Marvel not that I said unto thee, Ye must be born again' (John 3.5-7).

In John 19.39 Nicodemus assisted Joseph of Arimathea with the entombment of Jesus, bringing one hundred pounds of mixed myrrh and aloes for his embalming. According to the Gospel of Nicodemus he then came out openly as a disciple and sheltered Joseph of Arimathea in his house. In the legend that concerns us Nicodemus himself became the object of persecution, being excommunicated by the Sanhedrin, whipped and deprived of all his worldly goods. Gamaliel, the great Rabbi and teacher of Saint Paul, took him charitably into his house. Inconsolable at the death of Jesus, despite all his own misfortunes, Nicodemus, wishing to immortalise in an image his memory of the Crucifixion, tried his utmost to carve and paint it. Finally, weary and discouraged, he fell asleep over his work and an angel came from heaven and completed it for him.

This sculpture was entrusted by Nicodemus on his deathbed to his loyal follower, Issachar, (Issac? cf. **Fécamp**) who hid it in his house, where for generations it was venerated in secret. During the iconoclastic period (725-842), when all sacred images in the Byzantine Empire risked destruction, Selenco, a devout Christian, who was the guardian of the Holy Face at the time, sold it for safe-keeping to an Italian Bishop, Gualfredo or Walfried, who had been told in a vision to seek it in the hospice of Ramleh. (Coincy-Saint Palais guesses that Nicodemus' refuge of Ramleh may have been Ramoth Gilead, the mountain of Galahad.) The sacred object was taken to the port of Joppa/Jaffa and put to sea in a vessel which, driven by divine power alone, arrived by a long and tortuous route in the mouth of the River Magra near Luni on Good Friday in 742 (see **Sarzana** and **Bocca di Magra**). The Bishop of **Lucca**, warned of its arrival in a dream, hastened to Luni to save it from the attentions of the locals who made a living from the wrecks that washed up on their shore. The boat itself was, however, already taking evasive action by rising into the air.

When the bishop examined the sculpture, he found that two phials of Holy Blood were hidden in the neck of the image. The Bishop of Lucca and his company brought the vessel safely to shore and exerted pressure on the Bishop of Luni, so that each city received one of the phials. The Holy Face itself was placed in a cart drawn by two oxen, new to the yoke (cf **Heiligenblut**), who set off with it for Lucca. At first the image was placed in the church of Saint Frigidian (Frediano), a sixth-century missionary from Ulster. In 930 the image disappeared from San Frediano three times to the garden of the church of Saint Martin, where a sanctuary was built for it and where it remains to this day inside the Cathedral.

Historically, there is no doubt that the Holy Face has been in its secure octagonal chapel, of green, white and gold, since 1119. Famously, the somewhat heretical and diabolical King William Rufus II of England (ruled 1087-1100) considered no oath binding unless sworn by the Holy Face of Lucca. And it was long a favourite pilgrimage for the Normans (cf. **Fécamp**). In 1109 the Duke of Bohemia sent gifts to the image. Pope Urban II prayed to it for the success of the First Crusade and later pilgrims to it included Dante, Saint Bruno and the two great saints of Siena, Bernadino and Catherine.

There is no questioning its fame throughout Christendom in the Middle Ages. Copies of it were installed in Pisa, Pistoia, Siena, Naples, Messina, Venice, Bologna, Brescia, Cremona, Genoa, Rome, Prague, Avignon, Marseilles, Paris, Lyons, Geneva, Noli, **Valencia**, **Madrid**, **London**, **Portugal**, Holland and as far afield as India and China.

The image poses many problems. One of the very few Black Christs in Europe, it is also exceptionally large—2.5 metres high—and quite unlike any other image of Christ, although art-historians claim that it could be stylistically assigned to the eleventh century.

Today, although the Holy Face is in San Martino, the chapel of the Holy Blood is still in San Frediano, the second chapel on the right from the front. San Frediano also houses a fresco of the sixteenth century by Amico Aspertini, showing the Volto Santo in the ox-cart being carried by the divine will from Luni towards Lucca. Some, however, claim that the Holy Blood is still hidden near its original hiding-place in the Volto Santo, not far from the brain of Christ (but cf. **Bocca di Magra**).

—Mantua—

Maps 428 G14 and 988 fold 14

Mantua is an ancient city, as mantic as its name, founded by Manto, daughter of the prophet Tiresias. Mantua was also the birth-place of Virgil, believed to be of Celtic descent, who married Magia, the daughter of Magius. He was considered the greatest magician as well as the greatest poet of the Roman world, who prophesied the coming of Christ.

For us Mantua is the city of Longinus who wielded the magical Spear of Destiny (see **Vienna** and **Zöbingen**) and caused blood and water to flow from the side of Christ. It is the only city in Christendom to claim his tomb, which can be visited in the last chapel on the right before the transept in the Basilica of Sant' Andrea. The centurion was cured of blindness by the Holy Blood at the crucifixion and was the first to proclaim Christ as the Son of God.

The name Longinus is derived from the Greek word for 'lance' and it seems likely that he took on, in the Europe of the Dark Ages, some of the attributes of two magician gods who wielded an invincible lance, Lug for the Celts and Wotan for the Teutons. The lance, dripping blood, accompanies the Grail from its first appearance. The heroic avatar of both Lug and Wotan, is Lancelot (cf **Sées**, **Saint Fraimbault** and **Senlis**). Longinus brought some of Christ's blood to Mantua, where he was martyred in AD 37.

This blood is still the centre of an important cult in the crypt chapel of the Basilica. It is preserved in a sanctuary that can only be opened by eleven keys, held separately by various representatives of the church and the city. The relic is exposed only on Good Friday. On the door of the sanctuary in the crypt is an image of what appears to be Mary Magdalen holding a large chalice. Above, in glass cases, can be seen two facsimiles of the gilt glass-fronted flasks that contain the Holy Blood. *(See Plate 20)*

In the chapel of Longinus, he is depicted in an engraving on the front of his sarcophagus holding the lance in his left hand and raising a radiant vessel of the Holy Blood in his right. In the large painting to the right of the tomb he is shown kneeling at the foot of the cross, Grail in hand. On a large marble tomb, surrounded by a railing, in the transept near the entrance to the crypt, where people throw coins for good luck, is an unusual carving of the symbols of the Crucifixion—cross, hammer, nails and pliers surmounted by a Grail—resurrection triumphing over death. *(See Plate 19)*

That the Grail and Spear, the cosmic womb and phallus, belong together is emphasised by the presence across the road from Sant' Andrea in the beautiful

Piazza delle Erbe of the eleventh-century Rotonda di San Lorenzo, the round church of the Grail saint, Lawrence.

The cult of Saint Longinus was forgotten for many centuries until, in AD 804, Saint Andrew (cf **Saint Maurice**) appeared to a pious woman and showed her the site of the tomb. So many miracles resulted from the discovery of the relic of the Holy Blood that Pope Leo III encouraged Charlemagne to go to Mantua and verify its authenticity (cf **Charroux**).

During a period of troubles in the tenth century, the relic was hidden, to be rediscovered again by a blind man called Adalbert, about the time of the celebration of the birth of Matilda of Canossa in 1046 who, as the great Countess of Tuscany, established the prosperity of **Modena** and upheld the Pope against the Emperor. The fourth Duke of Mantua, Vincenzo de Gonzaga, founded in 1608 with papal blessing the order of the Knights of the Redeemer or of the Precious Blood, with twenty members and a Grand Master. In 1635 the Order of the Sisters of the Precious Blood was established. The direct line of the Gonzagas passed to the Dukes of Nevers. The family provided two Grand Masters or Nautonniers of the Prieuré de Sion, the order established to defend the hypothetical royal bloodline of Jesus and Mary Magdalen.

—Modena—

Maps 428 114 and 988, fold 14

From the Grail seekers' point of view Modena is chiefly notable for the remarkable early carvings over the Porta della Pescheria on the north side of the cathedral of San Gemignano. Some scholars believe that these carvings date from 1120—1140, in which case they are contemporary with Geoffrey of Monmouth's *Historia Regum Britanniae,* and much earlier than the publication of stories of Guinevere's abduction. The archivolt shows how early such tales became popular in Italy (cf **Otranto**).

The scene depicts Guinevere (named Winlogee) held captive in a castle by Mardoc (probably Mordred) but literally, Marduk, the Babylonian god who overthrew the original feminine chaos-deity Tiamat. Other figures, Artus de Bretani, Galvagin (Gawain), Che (Kay), Isdennus (Yder) and Galvarin, are trying to rescue her.

—Orvieto—

Map 430, fold N18

Word made Flesh, the bread of nature,
By His Word to Flesh He turns;
Wine into His Blood He changes.

(PANGI LINGUA, SAINT THOMAS AQUINAS)

We visited the chapel of the Corporal (see **Bolsena**) in Orvieto Cathedral on 5 April. Not until we returned to London did we discover that this was the feast of Saint Juliana of Liège, whose visions and lobbying had from 1230 created a groundswell in favour of a new feast for the universal Church, that of Corpus Christi, which celebrates on the Thursday after Trinity Sunday the continuing real presence of Christ in the world. Maundy Thursday would have been an obvious date for such a celebration, but Juliana's vision of the full moon, with one small segment still dark, convinced the authorities that a special new date was required, separate from the drama of Easter week. Pre-eminent among these authorities was James Pantaleon, Archdeacon of Liège and a fervent supporter of Juliana, who, as Urban IV, was the Pope who happened to be in Orvieto at the time of the Holy Blood miracle at **Bolsena**. He died in 1264 after a papacy of only three years, but it was his bull *Transiturus* which instituted the observance of the new feast of Corpus Christi. The wonderful cathedral of Orvieto (whose construction was ordered by Urban IV) was begun in 1290 to house the relics of **Bolsena** and is the major and oldest ecclesiastical building celebrating the miraculous presence of Christ in the Eucharist.

It also happened that Saint Thomas Aquinas, one of the greatest theologians and poets of the Church, was present in Orvieto at the time of the **Bolsena** miracle and was commissioned by the Pope to write the divine office for the new feast, which included the two magnificent hymns *Lauda Sion* and *Pange Lingua*.

La Porta del Corporale was specially built for the ceremonial entry of the relic into the church. Above the doorway is a sculpture depicting the miracle and an inscription of the words: 'In corporale videt miraculum'. The Chapel of the Corporal is situated in the north transcept, behind the sixteenth-century organ. The relics of the corporal with the Holy Bloodstains are kept in the splendid tabernacle, flanked by two angels, which was designed by Nicola da Siena in 1358 and completed by Orcagna. The reliquary itself is made of silver-gilt and translucent enamel and was created by the Sienese Ugolino di Vieri in 1337. The life of Christ and the account of the miracle are sculpted on it.

If you travel from Orvieto to **Bolsena** you will get a breathtaking view of this medieval hill-top city.

—Otranto—

Map 431, fold G37

The earliest representation in colour of King Arthur is to be found in Otranto Cathedral (cf **Modena**). There the entire floor consists of an enormous mosaic showing the signs of the zodiac, the labours associated with each month, various biblical scenes, particularly the stories of Adam and Eve, Noah and Cain and Abel. Intermingled with these are hunting scenes, a whole medieval bestiary and the portraits of Alexander the Great, Solomon, Constantine and Arthur. All these are situated on the great central Tree of Life. Though, curiously, a second tree grows robustly at the top of the picture out of the Grail, borne by an angel in the sign of Aquarius. The angel is pouring water into a Tau-cross, held by a woman, with a cauldron hanging at the foot of it. Immediately to the right, on the other side of the main tree, above the sign Pisces, King Arthur, designated as Rex Arturus, bestrides a curious animal, like a large billy-goat, confronting confidently a panther-like beast. In his left hand he holds a long-handled sceptre while his right hand is raised as though greeting Adam and Eve being expelled from Eden by an angel. *(See Plate 23)*

The mosaic, which is a remarkable work of esoteric teaching, was made in 1163-5 by the priest Pantaleone at the request of Archbishop Jonathan in what was at that time an important point of departure for crusaders from this Norman kingdom. The pavement is normally cordoned off so that close examination is difficult and no photography is allowed. When we arrived, however, on Easter Sunday, a vast congregation leaving the Basilica at the end of archiepiscopal High Mass, opened for us a window of opportunity to spend ten minutes to stand on the ancient mosaic, gazing and photographing to our hearts' delight.

—Pisa—

Maps 428 K13 and 988, fold 14

The Pisans, during the First Crusade, obtained from Daimberto, the Patriarch of Jerusalem, who was also their bishop, and from Godefroy de Bouillon, some bodies of saints to take back to their cathedral, amongst which was that of Nicodemus. It was installed in the last chapel on the right before the transept. The inscription testifies to his presence in this tomb:

> *Gamalielis Nichodemi Et Abiae Patris Filiii Ac*
> *Nepotis Vt Ecclesia Docat Civivm Terrene Ac*
> *Coelestis Hiervsalem Foelici Tempore PisanoR*
> *Tradvcta Cadavera Marmore Sub Hoc Novato Recondivntvr*

Who is this Nicodemus, a strict Pharisee and ruler of the Jews, with a Greek name meaning Victory of the People, who came to Jesus secretly by night asking the vital question about rebirth, and was he the co-founder of the Grail tradition with Joseph of Arimathea?

Although famous for his wealth in Jerusalem and a member of the Sanhedrin, he risked and lost all by defending Jesus and assisting Joseph of Arimathea to embalm the body of the Crucified, laying it in a new tomb. He had the reputation, like Wotan and other magicians, of being a blacksmith. He removed the nails from the hands and feet of Christ, and is shown in art at the feet of the body, near Saint Mary Magdalen, having brought one hundred pounds of spices to be placed in the shroud. According to the legend he left the *Volto Santo* to Gamaliel, who left it to Zacchaeus of **Lucca**, who left it to James, who left it to Simon. It may be that Nicodemus is actually Simon in whose house Mary Magdalen anointed Christ's feet, with an unguent that contained the Holy Foreskin, and wiped them with her hair.

—Ravello—

Map 431, fold P25

Wagner was working on his Grail opera *Parsifal* when he arrived in Ravello on 26 May 1880. As soon as he saw the Villa Ruffolo he exclaimed: 'The magic garden of Klingsor has been found!', words which he then inscribed in the visitor's book of the Hotel Palumbo. He surely was led to this conclusion not just by the enchantment of the garden and its magnificent view over the mountains of the Sorrento peninsula and the Bay of Salerno, but by the brooding presence of the eleventh-century tower that presides over the ensemble. Water and small grottoes abound and in the gate-tower at each corner stand four statues—two 'grail-maidens' and two old men with the mien of wizards. Wagnerian concerts are held each summer in this magical garden of Klingsor, whence Parsifal retrieved the sacred spear which had wounded Amfortas. With this lance he healed the old Fisher King whom he then succeeded as guardian of the Grail. *(See Plate21)*

Ravello has other associations, more venerable and tangible, to the Holy Blood. The cathedral contains the blood of Saint Pantaleon, the protector of Ravello. Annually, on 27 July, the blood liquefies within its ampulla and remains clear, crimson and bubbly until the Feast of the Holy Cross on 14 September. In 1579 the vessel was cracked when a priest held a candle too close to it but no drop of blood has escaped from that day to this and the miracle was not affected.

The relic is contained in a sanctuary beneath the painting of the Saint tied to an olive tree, which burst into leaf on contact with his body. He is accompanied by one of his hermetic teachers, Saint Hermolaos. The chapel to the left of the High Altar was filled with flowers and light and open for prayer until 11.45 pm on Maundy Thursday, Grail-night, the Feast of the Last Supper. The sacristan assured us that the blood of Saint Pantaleon, now preserved in a convent in Madrid, came originally from Ravello (see San **Pantaleón de Losa**, **Madrid**, **Weingarten** and **Saint Denis**).

The House of Anjou, the Grail family, had a predilection for Ravello, and Charles II and his successor, Robert the Wise, stayed at the Villa Ruffolo. So did the only English pope, Hadrian IV, born Nicholas Breakspeare.

SCALA

1.5 km above Ravello stands what is now the village of Scala that once rivalled its powerful neighbour in importance. In its Cathedral of Saint Lawrence are preserved relics of the saint who sent the Holy Grail on its long journey to **San Juan de la Peña** and **Valencia**. His story is depicted in a series of frescoes on the ceiling.

—Rome—

Map 430, fold Q19 (includes town plan)

As travellers to Italy soon find out, all roads lead to and from Rome. So it is with relics of the Holy Blood, Holy Grail and Spear of Destiny. As our book is not much concerned with museums and monuments in large capital cities, we have been very selective with the sites pertaining to the Quest in Rome.

Raphael's stanza in the *Vatican* records the miracle of the Holy Blood at **Bolsena** and Fra Angelico's fresco shows Pope Sixtus II giving the Holy Grail to Saint Lawrence. At *Saint Peter's* there is preserved a statue of Longinus, commemorating the fact that the Spear of Destiny once resided here. What is claimed to be the reliquary of the Holy Foreskin is in the Vatican Museum (see **Calcata**).

At *Saint John in Lateran,* the earliest official residence of the popes, is an ancient, yellowish, jasper chalice, which has been associated with the Grail and may be the one that Saint Jerome brought from Jerusalem to Rome in the fifth century. Here, too, the Holy Foreskin of **Calcata** was originally housed. There are seven churches dedicated to Saint Lawrence, one of which, *San Lorenzo in Panisperna,* is built over the spot where he was martyred on his gridiron. Nearby in the church of *Santa Prassede,* in the chapel known as the garden of paradise, is a short marble column to which Christ was tied for his flagellation and on which the first shedding of the Holy Blood during the Passion took place.

Two sites stand out for us as notably connected to the Grail legend: one legendary and miraculous and the other part of the acknowledged history of the church.

ST JOHN AT THE LATIN GATE

It was here that the beloved disciple drank from a poisoned chalice and emerged unharmed from a cauldron of boiling oil to proceed to Patmos where he wrote his Revelation. The Basilica of Saint John is a rare oasis within the walls of Rome where one can park one's car unhindered and stroll quietly through the gardens. No wonder it is a favourite place for fashionable Romans to marry and for a pre-nuptial retreat with the Rosminians, whose college is attached to it. When we arrived from Frascati we found the Via Latina one way in the wrong direction (but when in Rome do as the Romans) and the Basilica was shut by the police. Seeing a priest supervising the unloading of furniture into the Collegio Missionario we asked him if the small octagonal building, just within the gate, was where Saint John had undergone his baptism of fire and spirit. Without a word he handed us the key, indicating that we should drop it through the letter box when we had finished.

The building of 1508 is dedicated in French to the pleasure of God, and replaces a medieval chapel. It contains wall-paintings showing Saint John drinking from a chalice with a rampant serpent and emerging unharmed from the vessel of boiling oil. Interestingly, Pope Adrian I (772-795), the first restorer of the Basilica, dedicated it to Saint John the Baptist, although it had long been a titular church to John the Evangelist. Surely the Pope knew what he was doing and wished to emphasise the importance of the continuity of baptism for the Christian soul from that of water to that of the spirit. Rudolph Steiner believed that both Saint Johns, from midsummer and midwinter, formed one soul with Lazarus as the beloved of Christ.

ST LAWRENCE WITHOUT THE WALLS

St Lawrence Without the Walls, off the Via Tiburtina, one of the major roads leading out of Rome to the east, is very much less peaceful than Saint John of the Latin Gate, although it is the site of one of the great Roman cemeteries. It was here that Saint Lawrence was buried. Frescoes in the narthex show him handing the Grail to the Spanish legionary who would take it to Huesca, the first stage of its journeyings to **San Juan de la Peña** and **Valencia**. The paintings, which were badly damaged by allied bombing in 1943, have been well restored and depict all the events of the life of the saint.

—Sarzana—

(Basilica of Santa Maria)
Maps 428, fold 36, J 11 and 988 fold 14

The story of the arrival of the Precious Blood at Sarzana is a curious one, though not unfamiliar (cf **Fécamp**). Nicodemus, the rich ruler of the Pharisees, who came to Jesus secretly by night, asked him what deserves to be counted as a true Grail question: 'How can a man be born again when he is old?' The full legend of the Holy Face which he carved, the phials of Blood which he hid in the neck, and his burial, can be found under **Lucca** and **Pisa**. The part that concerns Sarzana began with the arrival in 742, amid various signs and wonders, of a boat containing this precious cargo, in the mouth of the river Magra (see **Bocca di Magra**).

The chapel of the Precious Blood, to the right of the chancel in the Cathedral, is dominated by the tabernacle containing the phial of the Blood of Christ which is exposed for veneration only on July 14 and 15. Above, there is a painting of angels bearing the phial, while the silver door of the sanctuary depicts Christ at the Last Supper holding the chalice.

—Venice—

Map 988, fold 5 and 429, fold 14

The most precious relics in the Treasury of the Basilica of San Marco, including the flask containing the Precious Blood of Christ and the head of John the Baptist, were preserved in the great fire of 1231. One of eight special crystals, carved in the reign of Charles the Bald, which, if Flavia Anderson is correct, may be considered as genuine grails, is also to be found here.

In the late-fifteenth-century marble tabernacle of the church of the Frari a particularly tender relic, taken from Constantinople and donated to the church by Melchiore Trevisan in 1479, combines a drop of Christ's blood with some of the unguent with which Mary Magdalen anointed his feet.

Germany, Denmark, Austria, Slovena, Czech Republic, and Switzerland

Helsingør

Copenhagen

Denmark

Hamburg

Brunswick

Hildesheim Magdeburg

Externsteine

Cologne Wartburg

Aachen

Germany

Karlstein Prague

Ansbach Nuremberg Czech Republic

Zöbingen Wolframs Neukirchen beim Heiligenblut

Trifels Eschenbach

Neuschwanstein,

Hohenschwangau Vienna

Weingarten and Linderhof Herrenchiemsee

Basel Austria

Reichenau

Arlesheim/Dornach Heiligenblut

Switzerland Gurk

Ptuj

St Maurice Rogaska Slatina

Slovenia

Germany

*

—Aachen—

Map 987, fold 23

As the capital of Charlemagne's empire, Aachen played host to many of the most notable relics in Christendom. These included the Precious Blood, the head of the Spear of Destiny in the hilt of Charlemagne's sword and the Holy Prepuce (cf **Charroux**). The cathedral treasury, still one of the richest in Europe, includes many magnificent reliquaries and the chest of Richard of Cornwall (1209-72) (cf **Hailes Abbey**), which contained the four holy things, one of which was a particle of the Blood. The treasury also contains an Egyptian funerary urn considered in the Middle Ages to be a pot from Cana of Galilee in which Jesus transformed water into wine (cf **Reichenau**).Frederick II (see **Castel del Monte**) was crowned in **Aachen** in 1215.

—Ansbach—

(Saint Gumpert's Church)

Map 987, fold 26

We journeyed to the old Hohenzollern stronghold of Ansbach, mainly in search of the head of Lazarus, but the reference we had read was a mistake as it is kept in **Andlau**.

The chapel of the Swan Knights, an order founded by the Elector of Brandenburg in 1440, is, nevertheless, of considerable interest. Notable are the many winged skulls on the walls.

The original Swan Knight, Lohengrin, came from the pen of Wolfram, whose home, **Wolframs Eschenbach**, is 16km to the south-east.

—Brunswick/Braunschweig—

(The Onyx Vessel)

Map 987, fold 16

Brunswick is the traditional home of that greatest of German tricksters, Till Eulenspiegel, but the tricks he played on us were entirely beneficent. We had hoped to write our entries as we went along on a laptop PC, and the first trick was that we left the lead in London. We had no luck in replacing it in Hamburg, but were given the address of a firm in Brunswick who might be able to help. Trick number two: the Autobahn exits to Hildesheim being closed, we decided rather disconsolately to drop in to the computer firm at Brunswick en route to **Magdeburg**, though we knew that the museums we were interested in would be shut, as it was a Monday. It took us a long time to find the firm, weaving in and out of two breweries, gasping with thirst in the extreme heat, but with never a pub in sight. The man we needed was out to lunch and by the time he got back to inform us that our quest was in vain we decided to go and have a drink and a bite to eat at the station, asking the tourist office if they could give us any information about the Grail we knew to be in Brunswick. We were given the telephone number of Doctor Alfred Walz at the Herzog Anton Ulrich Museum. Not very encouraged, we telephoned him and explained to him why we wanted to see the Onyx Vessel. He invited us to come over to the museum straight away and said that he personally would show us the Vessel, which would not be on view again to the public until the following year (1993). Doctor Walz turned out to be the most patient and charming of guides; not only did he allow us to photograph this unique Vessel (also known as the Hochzeit Schüssel—marriage vessel) from all angles, but he also had photocopies made of important documents relating to the history of the vase. *(See Plate 13)*

The Vessel shows an amazingly intricate and skilful relief in the various layers of the onyx, portraying the youthful god Triptolemos of Eleusis, who, with Demeter and Fortuna, rides across the earth in a carriage pulled by two winged serpents, as well as Priestesses and women bringing offerings. This portrays, most likely, members of the Roman royal family as divine beings. The date of the Vessel is uncertain, but according to its style it probably originates from the times of the Emperors Claudius or Nero.

The history of the Onyx Vessel is troubled and its survival remarkable, as though it had a life of its own and will to survive. The first mention of it appears in 1542 in the inventory of the estate of the late Countess Isabella of **Mantua**. It is not known how the Vessel, believed to be a relic from the Temple of Solomon in Jerusalem and a container for something precious, came to **Mantua** and into the possession of the ruling Gonzaga family. In about 1630, with the end of the Gonzaga lineage, it fell into the hands of Franz Albrecht, Duke of Lauenburg. In 1641 he gave it to the owner of The White Lion Inn in **Venice** in order to find a suitable buyer. But the Duke died in 1642, before the Vessel was sold, and a desperate fight over who should be its rightful owner, ensued. Both the Emperor and the Doge got involved in this fierce dispute, but, finally, the Duke's widow, Christine Margaret, was officially declared the owner. Under a shroud of secrecy the Vessel was shipped, hidden in a barrel, to Hamburg where on 4 October 1644 the Countess' secretary took delivery of it.

The Countess also failed to find a buyer for the Vessel before her death in 1666. It now passed to her sister, the Duchess of Brunswick. Ferdinand Albrecht, the Duchess' son, inherited it upon her death. From now on it increasingly attracted the attention of scholars. This Onyx Vessel, measuring only 15.3cm in height and 6.5cm in width at its widest point, turned out to be a Hellenistic relic of the cult of Demeter, who presided over the mysteries of rebirth at Eleusis.

Ferdinand Albrecht died in 1687, but it took twenty-five years before his descendants could agree about the inheritance. In the meantime the Vessel remained hidden from view. A further twenty-three years on and Ferdinand Albrecht's wish came true when his son, Ferdinand Albrecht II, inherited it. But it was not until eighty years later that his estate could be fairly divided, owing to the increasingly high price placed upon the Onyx Vessel. Eventually, his grandson, Duke Carl I, became the new owner of it in 1767, and he began to exhibit it in the Museum of Brunswick, which he founded. Forty years later it escaped the plunderings of Napoleon's troops, the Duke's family having already fled with the Vessel to safety. Their journey took them via Denmark and Sweden to England. In 1815 the Vessel finally returned to the museum.

Its troubles were not over yet. During the revolution of 1830, the castle and museum were severely damaged by fire and the Vessel was considered destroyed. But after the exiled Carl II's death in Switzerland in 1873, the Vessel was found to have been in his possession all along and was eventually, after serious disputes with the authorities of Geneva, returned to Brunswick. In the 15th century a festival called the Grail took place here every seven years until it was forbidden by law in 1481.

—Cologne/Köln—

Map 412, fold D14

One of the most surprising doctors of the Church was Albertus Magnus, the greatest European natural scientist of his day as well as a notable wonder-worker and the teacher of Saint Thomas Aquinas. While Prior of the Dominicans in Cologne he entertained the Emperor to an al fresco Grail feast served by angels in the cloister garden in perfect weather while all around were the snow and ice of January. He also had a talking head that could answer any question. It was he who installed the relics of those Grail-bearers who are the symbol of **Cologne**, the three Kings, in the cathedral, of which he laid the foundation stone.

—The Exsternsteine—

Map 412, fold 111
Follow signs from Horn

This fantastic group of rocks, rising to 38m above a lake in a clearing of the Teutoburger Wald, is the sacred centre of the Germanic mysteries. Here, in AD 6, at the apogee of Roman power, Herrmann destroyed two legions under Varus in defence of the Teutonic palladium. Seven and a half centuries later it was the goal of Charlemagne's thirty-seven-year-long crusade against the Saxons, still faithful to the old religion, whose holy tree, Irminsul, stood nearby until the Christian armies destroyed it, though its horned shape can still be made out on the right hand side of the Descent from The Cross. To the renewed Grail cult of Rudolf Steiner and his followers, the boulders that time and war cannot destroy, represent the centre of Grail energy in Germany. *(See Plate 16)*

No one can now tell how the gods were honoured here, but the stones' name suggests that astrology was the corner-stone of the cult rendered (*Eck* corner, *Stern* = star, *Steine* = stones). This is borne out by the chapel perched high on one of the rocks where a round hole in a niche above a small pagan-looking altar is designed to admit the rays of the rising sun at the winter solstice.

The remarkable and unique sculpture (5 x 5.5m) of the Descent from the Cross, carved in the living stone next the entrance to the lower grotto chapel, shows a sun and moon in mourning either side of the Crucified. The two earliest heroes of Grail Christianity, Nicodemus and Joseph of Arimathea, are the central figures of the relief with Jesus, whose body is being passed by the one on to the shoulders of the other. God the Father, shown from the waist up, stands above his son, holding the soul of Christ and a triple banner surmounted by a knightly cross. Mary—whose head (now destroyed) is leaning against the head of Christ, which she cradles in her hands—and John, complete the group. At the foot of the cross, on a lower plane, Adam and Eve contend with a demonic dragon. The carving dates from about 1130, at the beginning of the interest in things Arthurian. Evidence points to the existence of a hermitage on the site since *c.* 1100.

Outside the main complex, looking west, is a replica of the Holy Sepulchre in Jerusalem, containing a stone sarcophagus.

Entry to the grotto chapel and the hermit's cell is not permitted, so we were unable to inspect the pre-Christian runes that have been found there. One of them in the form of a double gallows recalls both Wotan, the Gallows-God, and the repeated rune symbol for the winter solstice.

—Hildesheim—

Map 987, fold 15

Hildesheim became the capital of German Romanesque art and architecture under the Emperor Otto 1(912-973); it is also the point from which the knowledge and cult of Longinus radiated throughout Germany. This was thanks to the magnificent bronze doors of the cathedral, commissioned by Bishop Bernward (*c.* 1015). Here Longinus is depicted as an ageing figure on foot with a short primitive lance piercing the right armpit of Christ, while the Crucified turns towards him, meeting his fading vision with a penetrating and healing gaze. The sponge-bearer on the other side is raising up to Jesus his anaesthetising draft in a vessel on the end of a pole.

The Cathedral owed its foundation to the dream of Charlemagne's son, Ludwig the Debonnaire, in 815, in which the Golden Madonna of the Rose (now in the museum) revealed herself to him. The rose is still there, proudly covering the Lady Chapel up to 9m. It was believed destroyed with eighty per cent of the Cathedral and most of the town by air attacks in 1945, but burst into flower again eight weeks later.

—Magdeburg—

Map 987, fold 16

Magdeburg (city of the maid) traces its legendary origins to Charlemagne, wielder of the victorious Spear of Destiny, who made it the easternmost stronghold of the Reich against the Slavs. Historically it was the place chosen by the Emperor Otto I as his wedding present to his wife Edith with its monastery of Saint Maurice, founded in 937. Edith, daughter of King Edmund I of England, died here on 26 January 946. Saint Maurice (d. 287 or 302), who was the first known possessor of Longinus' spear in the Christian era (see **Saint Maurice**), became the patron saint of German warriors. The Spear became renowned as a talisman of victory when Charles Martel used its power to save Europe from the Muslim invasion at **Poitiers** in 732.

Magdeburg was obliterated by bombs shortly before the end of World War II and then suffered the worst ravages of Stalinist architecture for the masses. The cathedral suffered appalling damage, and, although religious services have been held here since 1955, its restoration is still far from complete. One of its treasures has, however, survived more or less intact—the black-faced, red-lipped, thirteenth-century statue of Saint Maurice, clad in chainmail and breast-plate. *(See plate 17)* What is missing is the spear which he once gripped in his right hand. Curiously, the spear, or its head, has also been removed from the two other statues of the saint in the Dom. However, in the Ernstkapelle, a splendid fifteenth-century statue shows him with all accoutrements complete.

This is a rare representation of Saint Maurice with African colouring and features. It may be a memory of Christian knights from the upper Nile who took part in the Crusades. It raises questions as to what Maurice, the commander of the Theban legion from Gnostic Egypt, really represents.

It seems certain that the Spear of Destiny would have been at the side of Otto the Great when he resided in Magdeburg. That it is a Grail city is indicated by the play presented in 1280 featuring a character called Frau Feie (Sophia or Morgan-le-Fay) in which a tournament was held in a camp called the Grail.

—Neukirchen beim HeiIigenblut—

Map 413, V19, fold 21

In about 1400 in Louchim (Lautschim), 18km to the north-east across the bor-der into Bohemia, a Host was discovered on a tree-stump. This was treated as a miraculous event and a chapel was built on the site. The cult was quickly fused with, and indeed superseded by, that of the Black Virgin now venerated at Neukirchen.

This was a moment pregnant with revolution in Bohemia. Jan Huss (1369-1415) was inflaming the country with his social and religious reforming move-ment. He was particularly hostile to the pilgrims of Wilsnack where three consecrated hosts were said to have been found, unharmed but bloodstained, after the church there was destroyed by fire. So, it is not surprising that, after the execution of Huss for heresy at Constance, his followers, to whom he was by now a national hero as well as a religious leader, should have vented their wrath on sites such as Lautschim where transsubstantiation was glorified. The shrine and the Virgin were threatened, and a local woman, Susanna Halada, carried the statue to safety at what became Neukirchen beim Heiligenblut in Bavaria, and hid it in a lime tree, or in the chapel, where vestiges of an ancient tree-cult persisted.

But the Hussites had not forgotten the Virgin of Lautschim and during a foray across the border in 1450 a zealot of the cult, called Kretschma, discov-ered it and threw it three times down the nearby well (now in the right-hand side-altar in the church). Each time the statue re-emerged until, in rage and frustration, he finally smote its head with his cutlass. Fresh blood gushed forth from the wound leading us to the conclusion, though this is not stated in the tradition, that the original Host, discovered in 1400, had been inserted into the head of the Virgin. This would explain why the two cults—of the miraculous Host and the Black Madonna—have become one.

Now it was time for the image to strike back. Kretschma suddenly found that he was unable to escape—his horse refused to move and remained rooted to the spot. Suspecting that a spell had been cast by means of the horseshoes, he proceeded to wrench them off, one after another, all to no avail. Acknowledging his defeat Kretschma submitted to the superior power residing in the image and became converted into the most faithful servant of our Lady of Heiligenblut and her cult, frequently returning here on pilgrimage. From that day to this the pilgrimage has remained flourishing.

Neukirchen beim Heiligenblut is an attractive small town surrounded by gently sloping hills. To get the best view of the church and its setting take the path past the Stations of the Cross, through meadows and cornfields, to the wooded hilltop where the chapel of Saint Ann with its healing spring stands.

The pilgrimage church contains much that is worth seeing: nowhere else have we discovered two enchanting black cherubs (above the far left-hand side-altar). The wall-paintings, which tell the whole legend of Neukirchen beim Heiligenblut, from the discovery of the Host to the conversion of Kretschma, are full of interesting and vivid detail.

—Nuremberg/Nürnberg—

Map 987, fold 26

Nürnberg was, from 1424-1796 and 1938-46, the home of the Spear of Destiny and the other Regalia of the Empire. Napoleon attempted to seize the spear from Saint Katherine's church but it was removed to Habsburg lands and hidden until the danger had passed. Nürnberg was and remains the great centre of Germanism—which is why Hitler chose it for his greatest rallies and why the huge and magnificent German National Museum is still there. Dürer was a Nürnberger and painted two pictures of the annual Easter-tide exposition of the Spear and the other relics to public veneration. The Katharinenkirche was destroyed in 1945 and the partially-restored ruins are now used for concerts and as an extension of the National Library. According to Ravenscroft, it housed the Spear again during the Second World War.

The same author notes that the USA became the new claimants to the Spear of Destiny at 2.10 pm on 30 April 1945. This was the precise moment when Hitler committed suicide in Berlin and US army intelligence discovered the Spear in a vault in Oberesschmiedgasse beneath Nürnberg Castle. At this point its power passed from Germany to America and President Truman was soon to OK the fateful decision to drop the atomic bomb on Japan. Later, rockets, also a German invention, armed with nuclear warheads, were to embody perfectly Wotan's Spear of Destiny and destruction, Gungnir.

—Reichenau—

Map 413, K23 and map 427, L2

We had no intention of spending the night in Reichenau but fate decided otherwise. A downpour and traffic jam at the frontier in Constance made us so late that our first thought on reaching the Holy Island in the Lake of Grace (Gnadensee) was to find a room for the night. Having done this we wandered into the Marienmünster, which was bustling with activity in preparation for the Feast of the Assumption. We importuned the busy sacristan who was to prove an invaluable ally to us. He allowed us behind the altar to examine and photograph the remarkable wall paintings, portraying the legend of the Holy Blood at Reichenau.

We then wandered across to the small Drogerie on the other side of the road and discovered a brand-new guide, which had just appeared that week, recounting the legend of a precious relic, totally unknown to us, the water-pot from Cana of Galilee (Kana-Krug), preserved in the Abbey-treasury. This vessel, in which Jesus performed his first miracle of turning water into wine, at the sacred marriage in Cana, was surely a proto-Grail. *(See Plate 14)* We dashed back to the church, but by now it was closed. Next day we watched the parade of musicians and fusiliers in their late eighteenth-century uniforms of red and white, and the girls of the village who looked charming in their national dress and elaborate headgear.

As the procession of relics ended we became aware that the sacristy, with all its treasures, would not now be open for two days. We lay in ambush for the returning priests and, as soon as they were in the presbytery, for a well-deserved lunch, we rang the bell and confronted them with our outrageous request to be allowed to see the Kana-Krug and other relics. They could not have been kinder and gave us permission to tell the much-put-upon sacristan to let us in. He complied with great courtesy, despite the fact that an earlier visitor from Britain, in the last century, had stolen the ancient staff of the Abbot, which is now one of the treasures of the Victoria and Albert Museum.

The story of the Kana-Krug's presence in Reichenau **is** complicated and concerns an invincible, Lancelot-like, Greek knight called Symeon who performed great deeds for his own king and later for Charlemagne. Like many another Grail-Knight he left the profession of arms for the pursuit of sanctity and was granted by the Patriarch of Jerusalem one of the water-pots from Cana in his possession. The precious relic was stolen from Symeon who, like Parzival after his first Grail failure, vowed to devote his life to its rediscovery. The vessel itself had by now reached Galicia (where Galahad achieved the Grail—see **O Cebreiro**), and the king of the land, Dietrich, in desperate straits through his war with the king of the Franks, gave the Kana-Krug to Hatto, Archbishop of Mainz, to persuade him to act as mediator. Hatto took the vessel to the Abbey of Reichenau, which lay within his charge, and it was here that Symeon, after years of fruitless quest, was to find it. He settled here as a monk and ended his days on the island.

The story of the arrival of the Holy Blood in Reichenau is no less complicated than that of the Kana-Krug, with which indeed it seems to have become confused, from the time of the earliest text (799). The housebook of the abbey of Reichenau (tenth/eleventh centuries) perpetuates the contamination, so, for the sake of simplicity, having told the tale of Symeon and the Kana-Krug, we will now keep the tradition of the Holy Blood separate, though, on a symbolical level they have, of course, much in common.

Hassan, the prefect of **Huesca**, wished to ingratiate himself with Charlemagne by offering him a priceless gift if they could but meet. The gift was a vessel containing the Holy Blood of Christ. Such a scenario is not implausible: in his second invasion of Spain, Charlemagne penetrated little further than the **Huesca**-Barcelona line. **Huesca**, of all cities in Europe at that time, was the one most associated with the cult of Saint Lawrence's Grail. Hassan and his relics reached the island of Corsica where the prefect fell ill and implored the Emperor to come to him and receive the gifts from his hands. Charlemagne, nervous of sea travel, tried to persuade his adviser and chronicler, Einhart, to go in his place. But the monk was equally timorous. The task finally devolved on Waldo, the Abbot of Reichenau, and Hunfrid, the ageing lord of Istria. The gifts they brought back for Charlemagne from the dying prefect in Corsica were: a small onyx flask containing the Holy Blood and a small cross made from gold and precious stones, containing a piece of the True Cross as well as some of the blood of Christ. Of these the particle of the True Cross and the Holy Blood are still preserved in the reliquary of Reichenau.

Hunfrid, the faithful servant, granted a boon by Charlemagne, requested the very relic of the Holy Blood that he had brought to the Emperor, who reluctantly granted his wish. Hunfrid built a convent at Schänis, between the Walensee and the Zürich Obersee, where the relic was venerated until his death. His son, Adalbert, inherited it and, in time of war, fled with it to the ancestral domain of Istria. After many adventures the treasure came into the hands of Walther and Schwanhilde in exchange for the hand of their daughter to Ulrich, the great-great-grandson of Hunfrid. When Schwanhilde visited the monastery of Reichenau to pray, her accompanying chaplain, without her knowledge, had brought the Holy relic with him. Schwanhilde, constrained by bad health and in fear of her life, acceded to the requests of the monks, and left the relic with them, after which she made a complete recovery. The relic arrived at Reichenau on 7 November 925 and is kept today in the red tabernacle behind the baroque iron rood-screen in the church.

Stein makes the interesting point that the reign of Charlemagne marked the point of separation between esoteric Grail-Christianity, represented by Waldo of Reichenau, and dogmatic Catholic orthodoxy in the person of Einhart, who wrote the history of the period, making un-persons of whom he chose, picking up a juicy benefice as Abbot of **Saint Denis**, where he left his features on the door.

An old verse by Abbot Ermenrich von Ellwangen in the ninth century tells us that 'even in the misty land of the British, Reichenau is famous' 'weithin schallet dein Ruhm bis ins neblige Land der Britannen'. How many Britons have heard of it today?

The best time to visit Reichenau, if you wish to see the Holy Blood exposed, as well as the procession, is the day after Trinity Sunday.

Guided visits of the treasury are May to September ll—l2am and 3-4pm, closed Sundays and feast-days. Further information from the tourist office, telephone 0 75 34/2 76.

—Weingarten—

Map 987, fold 35/36 and map 413 LM23

Weingarten, one of the oldest and best-documented shrines of the Holy Blood, is also a Grail centre. It is of special interest to British visitors since it was Judith, whose first husband was Tostig, Earl of Northumbria, though she is often referred to as a Queen of England, who presented the relics to the Abbey in 1094. The most notable descendants in direct line, through the House of **Brunswick**, of her second husband, Welf IV, are the British Royal Family. The lion and unicorn coat of arms can still be seen on either side of the tomb of the Guelphs and on the coat of arms of the iron screen guarding it.

The funerary chapel also contains a painting of Longinus and it is to his reputed burial place of **Mantua** that we must return for the beginning of the story. In 804 the relic of the Holy Blood, which Longinus had brought with him from Jerusalem, and which had been buried in **Mantua**, was rediscovered. According to the Frankish annals, Pope Leo III, who had crowned the Emperor in Rome, thought this news of sufficient importance to travel all the way to Crécy near Reims, to inform Charlemagne in person. During the Hungarian invasions the relic was once more concealed, to be dug up, yet again, on 12 March 1048. News of this second discovery (see **Mantua**) was dispatched at once to Regensburg, where the Emperor Henry III, the newly elected Pope Leo IX and Duke Boniface of Lombardy were meeting to discuss the relations of church and state. All three went to **Mantua** to preside over the excavation of the relic from its hiding place. After much hard bargaining the major portion of the Holy Blood remained in **Mantua** while the Pope and the Emperor each received a small particle of it. Henry took his to Wurttemberg and on his death-bed, 5 October 1056, bequeathed it to Count Baldwin V of Flanders, known as the Pious, who was the step-father of Judith and great-grandfather of Thierry of Alsace, the recipient of the blood relic of **Bruges**.

Baldwin in his turn left the Precious Blood to his beloved step-daughter. It was Judith who, on 31 May 1090, four years before her death, entrusted it to the Abbey of Weingarten, founded by her, to solicit prayers for the safe return of her husband, Welf, from a journey to Jerusalem. The whole history is vividly illustrated in eight wall-paintings under the organ-loft.

Weingarten is the biggest baroque church in Germany and certainly looks it, perched as it is on its isolated promontory above the town. The relic of the Precious Blood is permanently exposed behind glass under the white-veined, red marble High Altar of 1718. Since 1956 the relic is kept in a splendid, most elaborate, golden Greek cross, surmounted by a smaller slimmer cross showing a dark-skinned, crucified Christ. In the middle of the lower cross can be seen a horseshoe-shaped, convex crystal and the cylinder containing the relic. This is surrounded by five layers of decoration, consisting of diamonds, emeralds, sapphires and rubies. The cross stands on the golden coat of arms of Weingarten, depicting the vines surrounding the church, and a golden chain with three gold rings is attached to this.

There are three other features which are peculiar to Weingarten. The first concerns the ritual riding of the relic in which hundreds of horsemen from the neighbouring countryside accompany a mounted priest who blesses the fields with it on Blood Friday, the day after Ascension. In 1753 there were 7000 and, even as recently as 1957, 2640 took part in the procession, which also includes about sixty brass bands, companies of musketeers with hundreds of standards and much of the population of Weingarten. The procession was authorised in 1529 as being 'a custom from time immemorial' and almost certainly dates back to a pre-Christian fertility practice. In another curious custom, wine was poured through an opening in the upper crucifix so that it flowed past the phial containing the blood, to be used both for priestly communion and in the cup offered to pilgrims. On every feast day it is exposed for the blessing of the sick at 6 pm.

Another tradition concerns the possible presence of the vessel of the Last Supper at Weingarten. According to Coincy-Saint Palais, the Abbey indicated that it possessed as a relic, first of all a chalice belonging to Christ and, secondly, a fragment of the cup in which his blood was preserved. The evidence for this is now mainly pictorial. An old engraving shows the Abbot Conrad von Wagenbach seated on his abbatial throne, holding in his right hand the blood-relic in order to heal a cripple, while his left hand seems to be offering direct contact with an orb or oval vessel to a kneeling pilgrim. It is this object which Coincy-Saint Palais takes to be the Holy Grail. A painting of Judith, priest-like, holding the vessel and linen in which the Holy Blood was preserved, shows her presenting this vessel to the Abbot of Weingarten.

The relic was hidden at various times in various places, most notably in 1215 with the Benedictine nuns of Höfen near Friedrichshafen, whose convent was dedicated to Saint Pantaleon (see **San Pantaleón de Losa** and **Ravello**). As to the form of the relic, it is said to be a piece of earth from Golgotha, lx35mm, soaked with the Holy Blood. Originally this had been preserved in the linen inside the vessel that Judith gave to Weingarten, but later the blood relic acquired a new container, and together with the linen was sent to Höfen. There the relic, which Coincy-Saint Palais states to be without doubt the first to be officially called the Holy Grail, was placed behind the statue of Saint Pantaleon, though in what form it was presented for veneration is not clear. It is noteworthy that Höfen came under the direction of the Abbey of **Reichenau** in 1140. Any connection between Weingarten and **Reichenau** is denied by Weingarten, though at **Reichenau** it is acknowledged that relics were exchanged between the two Abbeys. Undoubtedly both are Holy Blood sites, but it is now **Reichenau** which possesses the vessel in which Christ first turned water into wine. Höfen was destroyed in the fifteenth century and it could be assumed that whatever relics escaped destruction passed to **Reichenau.**

Another home of the Holy Blood, after it left its original linen cloth and vessel and before it was placed inside the crystal structure, is thought to have been inside a small, jewelled, enamelled enclosure on the golden, gem-studded cover of the missal of Abbot Berthold (1200-1232) which was made in Weingarten. It is now the property of the Pierpoint Morgan Library, New York.

—Wolframs Eschenbach—

Map 413, P19
16km south-east of Ansbach

Stratford-upon-Avon has Shakespeare, Alloway has Burns and Eschenbach has Wolfram and, since 1917, has added its greatest son's name to its own. No other poet of the Middle Ages has been so honoured—Robert de Boron is largely forgotten in **Montbéliard**, and in **Troyes** Chrétien has a street named after him but little else. In the Liebfrauenmünster, under its amazing multicoloured spire, with Wolfram's harp as centrepiece, you can see inside the entrance on the right, set into the wall, the purported tombstone of the poet. A relief shows Parzival on the left and his uncle, Amfortas, the wounded Fisher King, on the right, kneeling either side of an altar, while a dove makes its annual Good Friday descent to the Holy Grail bearing a Host in its beak. Ceiling bosses include the twin axes, which are Wolfram's coat of arms, and a rustic-looking Grail. The church contains a number of interesting polychrome wood-carvings: the Rosenkranz triptych, twice featuring the Grail-bearer Saint Lawrence (see **Huesca**), and another showing the discovery of the Holy Cross by Saint Helena.

The main square of the town is dominated by a statue of Wolfram, donated by the Emperor Maximilian II in 1861. The laurel-wreathed Minnesinger holds his harp in his hand and stands on a plinth in a fountain with a swan spitting water into it from each of the four corners reminding us that his poem ends with the story of the Swan-Knight Lohengrin. *(See Plate 15)* In nearby **Ansbach** the church of Saint Gumpert contains the chapel of the Swan-Knights. Wolfram himself was a member of the Teutonic Knights (Deutscher Ritterorden), closely linked to the Templars whom Wolfram proclaimed as the guardians of the Grail. The Teutonic Knights had a major commandery here preserved in the fine old Alte Vogtei Inn and in the Rathaus. The statue of Wolfram gazes towards a large Fachwerk (timbered) building, also pertaining to the order, which was reputedly his birthplace.

We were lucky to meet Anneliese Gössweir who, with her husband, runs the bookshop Besner and is the official custodian of the Wolfram cult here.

—Zöbingen—

Map 913, N20

Forty-five kilometres south-west of **Wolframs Eschenbach**, through attractive hills and woods, is the unassuming village of Zöbingen which lies just across the Bavarian border in Baden-Württemberg and claims to be the birthplace of Longinus, who held the Spear of Destiny and released the Precious Blood. In the nicest-looking pub on the crossroads at the end of the village the landlady pointed out to us his birthplace on the other side of the road to the right where a solid farmhouse now stands.

The Grail Castles of Germany

*

—Neuschwanstein—

Map 987, fold 36

Ludwig II of Bavaria (1845-86) lived only 102 days in this, the greatest of his castles built to celebrate the vision of the Grail he shared with Wagner. Then he was arrested by a commission from Munich on grounds of his irresponsible behaviour and taken to Berg Castle, where he drowned in the lake in mysterious circumstances. His great sin was his extravagance which nearly bankrupted his country. But all the great building operations of this last romantic monarch of Europe, the result of his visions of grandeur, must have been paid for many times over by the tourists who travel here from all over the world. In the rooms which he was able to complete he recreated brilliantly, through the eyes of Wagner and the group of artists and designers who flourished in Munich in the second half of the nineteenth century, the spirit of Wolfram von Eschenbach and the *Minnesänger* of seven centuries earlier. *(See Plate 11)*

What other Victorian building, except perhaps the Eiffel Tower, has known such success? One almost wishes it were less successful and that the pressures of conducted tours allowed more time to enjoy the wall-paintings of Wagner's operas and the poets of old. The Grail appears three times—most impressively when Parzival and his queen are depicted sending their son, Lohengrin, to rescue Elsa of Brabant. Ludwig seemed to have identified with Lohengrin when he called his fiance Elsa.

Earlier he had idealised Siegfried but later in life his hero was Parzival, the holy fool, humble and compassionate. He wanted Wagner to be his wise teacher, a Trevrizent. He wrote: 'I see in him the object of my existence'. Together they would give birth to the art of the future that would revive and celebrate the German genius of the *Minnesänger*—above all Wolfram von Eschenbach. His stated aim was to make Neuschwanstein a new Montsalvat for Wagner and himself.

Ludwig's intense interest in architecture began to show from the age of seven when he was given a set of building bricks by his grandfather, Ludwig I, to whom we owe many of the splendid buildings of Munich, and skilfully constructed a copy of the Holy Sepulchre and the Gate of Victory. Ludwig built Neuschwanstein, Grail castle of all Grail castles, on the pinnacle opposite his childhood home, **Hohenschwangau**. On this site once stood the castle of Schwangau (for which the whole county is named), centre, in the Middle Ages, of Swan Knights and *Minnesänger*.

—Hohenschwangau—

(Map 987, fold 36)

This home of ancient lineage
Looks far o'er alpine land …
And where Guelf, Stauff and Schyr
First drew their infant breath

Hohenschwangau, the castle below **Neuschwanstein**, built in the twelfth century by the Knights of Schwangau, became an important centre for *Minnesänger* in the Middle Ages. In the sixteenth century, after the last of the Schwangau Knights had died, the castle fell into disrepair. Maximilian II, father of Ludwig II and admirer of Wagner's *Lohengrin*, restored it during 1832-36 as a romantic Grail castle. The swan motif features in every one of the fourteen splendid rooms on view. It was here that Wagner was received by Ludwig and where he played for him on the 'Wagnerflügel' which still stands in the room of the Hohenstaufen The connection between the Hohenstaufen and the Wittelsbachs (Ludwig's family) is very close. It was one of Ludwig's ancestors, Count Otto of Wittelsbach, who rescued Barbarossa, Emperor Frederick I, and became in 1180 the first Wittelsbach Duke of Bavaria.

Here Ludwig II spent his happy, if lonely, childhood with his brother Otto. The beautiful interior of the castle with its magnificent furniture, decorations and frescoes of Germanic legends, including that of the Grail-Knight Lohengrin in the hall of the Swan Knights, as well as its unique setting above the two lakes—Alpsee and Schwansee—would have contributed much to the development of Ludwig's imagination and talent as an architect.

Although his father wanted him to become a good soldier, Ludwig would play with his puppet theatre instead and, isolated from the world outside, grew into a shy, unsociable youth who spent many hours in quiet contemplation, planning the building of his castles and reading works by Wagner, especially *Lohengrin.*

—Linderhof—

(Map 987, fold 36)

It appears that Linderhof, the only one of his castles that Ludwig saw completed, came into existence by pure accident. Ludwig had inherited an old hunting-lodge and wanted to add an extra bedroom. The result is this splendid castle with beautiful gardens, magical grottoes, fountains and a splendid Venusberg, legendary home of the Grail. The interior of Linderhof is breathtaking. This must be the most beautifully-decorated and furnished hunting-lodge castle in existence, even more sumptuous than the Trianon of Louis XIV which inspired it. One special feature is its 'Grail-table'. Ludwig could write his desired menu on a tablet, press a switch, and the table would disappear through the floor-boards, only to re-appear laden with whatever was asked for.

The *Blue Grotto* in the grounds was built to commemorate Wagner's opera *Tannhäuser.* This is the only artificially created grotto on such a scale. The theme of the huge painting behind the small lake is of Tannhäuser in Venusberg. A chronicler of Halberstadt in Saxony states: 'The historians are of the opinion that the Knight of the Swan came from the mountain where Venus lives in the Grail.' On the lake is Ludwig's golden shell-boat with its cupid figurehead. Ludwig himself would sit in it, drawn by a swan, like Lohengrin. At other times he would feed the swans with delicate, freshly-baked bread from a golden basket. *(See Plate 12)*

The *Venus Grotto, Hunding's Hut* and *Moorish Pavilion* are other sites that are a delight to visit at Linderhof.

—Herrenchiemsee—

(Map 987, fold 37)

The Isle of Herrenchiemsee had been the home of monks since at least 764. Ludwig 11(1845-1886) bought it after it had fallen into the most appalling state of disrepair and the church had been turned into a brewery. He installed model villages and moved in three hundred men and their families to work uninterruptedly on the building of this most splendid of all his castles from 1878 until the money ran out in 1885. Described by many as a second Versailles, it is not a copy of the French palace, although Ludwig was strongly influenced by the example of Louis XIV (whose son married the daughter of Elector Max Emanuel of Bavaria). Instead Ludwig developed his very own style and Herrenchiemsee 'is a German king's ideal of what royal architecture should be ...'

The golden Grail table, which is raised from the room below fully laden with all the dishes desired by his guests, is a feature we also met at **Linderhof**. In general, however, Ludwig eschewed social life and in the words of Bertram: '... here, in the world's most wonderful castle, the dreams of a solitary man, an idealist, have cast their spell over our spirit.'

—Trifels Castle—

(Map 304, fold 20)

Follow signs from Annweiler (5.6km) and allow 20 minutes for the climb from the car park.

The Michelin Green Guide, not much given to flights of fancy, states of the imperial castle that it 'housed the royal treasure, a fact which gives credit to the poetic tradition that it also once contained the Holy Grail.' In 1125 the Emperor Henry V, on his deathbed, ordered the Reichskleinodien (Imperial Regalia), now in the Hofburg of **Vienna**, to be placed in Schloss Trifels in the care of Duke Frederick, father of the Emperor Barbarossa, Germany's once and future king. They remained in Trifels, with some interruptions, until they came into the hands of the Habsburgs in 1274, after which they journeyed to Kyburg, home of the Habsburg family (1298-1325), Munich (1325), **Karlstein** (until 1424), **Nuremberg** (until 1806) and finally **Vienna**. Replicas of the regalia can now be seen in the restored castle, though not in the small royal chapel, still in its original state, which was their home in the twelfth century. If the Holy Grail was part of the regalia, it was presumably the Reichsapfel (orb), which lends support to Anderson's theory that it was a crystal fireball.

The importance of Trifels to the German myth is attested to by its elaborate reconstruction under the Third Reich. Much of the work was based on studies of the Emperor Frederick II's castles in Apulia (see **Castel del Monte**) and, in fact, Frederick himself was much interested in Trifels and built what is called the Palace there in the second quarter of the thirteenth century. King Ludwig II of Bavaria, the great castle builder, also took an interest in Trifels. The Bavarian government and the Trifels-Club, founded in 1866, stopped the castle being used as a quarry and spent large sums of money to preserve the ruins.

A further Grail connection is the slim silhouette of Scharfenberg Castle atop the next mountain. The Scharfenbergs were an important family: Konrad, who was Reich Chancellor and Bishop of Speyer in 1208, having for a time the regalia in his charge. Did Albrecht von Scharfenberg, who wrote in the second half of the thirteenth century *Der Jüngere Titurel,* which gives the most complete description of the Grail Castle, watch the construction of Frederick's new palace at Trifels?

For British visitors it is of interest that Trifels was where Richard Coeur de Lion was held prisoner in 1193, discovered by his faithful troubador, Blondel, and released for an unprecedented king's ransom of a quarter of all the money of England.

—Wartburg Castle, Eisenach—

(Map 412, N14)

Wartburg was the Grail castle of Wolfram von Eschenbach, author of *Parzival,* in the green heart of of Germany, the Thuringian Forest. The first castle was built by Ludwig the Leaper about 1067. It was his great grandson, Hermann I, Landgrave of Thuringia from 1192—1217, who established the bardic contest in 1207 known as the *Wartburgkrieg* and gained a reputation as a generous patron of poets and chivalry. His Minstrels' Chamber had room for a hundred, and the two most celebrated German poets of the period, Walther von der Vogelweide and Wolfram von Eschenbach spent much time at the Wartburg and enjoyed. Hermann's patronage. They both figured as protagonists in the poem *Wartburgkrieg* (written between 1230-1260). They maintained the primacy of Hermann for his hospitality and love of poetry against Heinrich von Ofterdingen, who supported the rival virtues of the Duke of Austria. 'Whoever should be the loser in the contest, which involved abstruse comparison between the sun, daylight, and the stars, would lose his head.

Ofterdingen, outnumbered by Hermann's supporters, summoned to his aid the magician Klingsor of Hungary (see **Ravello**) who knew each star by name. The Landgravine, Sophie, granted Ofterdingen a year's grace to bring Klingsor to the Wartburg where it was agreed that all would abide by his judgement. They arrived on 7 July and Klingsor predicted the birth of Saint Elizabeth of Hungary who was to spend two thirds of her short life, from 1211-1228, at the Wartburg before devoting her final three years to caring for the poor and sick of Marburg. Wolfram defeated the machinations of Klingsor by brandishing a crucifix. The story was immortalised in Wagner's opera *Tannhäuser*, the poet-knight who dwelt with Venus and the Holy Grail in the nearby Horselberg (see also **Linderhof**).

Although the Wartburg has suffered much from fire and decay it has been faithfully restored and never completely lost its place as the palladium of Germany. As well as housing her greatest poets and female saint of the thirteenth century it was to be the refuge where Luther, the father of the Reformation, translated the New Testament into German (1521-1522) and hurled his ink-pot at the devil. Goethe, who loved the Wartburg, staying there and sketching it in 1777, said of Luther's Bible: 'It was through Luther that the Germans became a nation'. The architect who restored the castle in the mid-nineteenth century, Hugo von Ritgen, echoed this sentiment: 'Germany achieved her spiritual identity on the Wartburg'.

Johann Sebastian Bach was born in its shadow in 1685, and a leader of those latterday Cathars, the Anabaptists, Fritz Erbe, died an agonizing death in its dungeon in 1548, having carved his name on the wall. He rejected the sacraments of both Catholic and Reformed Churches to the end. One of Germany's greatest painters, Lucas Cranach, the friend and portraitist of Luther, had connections with the Wartburg which houses some of his pictures, and a descendant of his was captain of the fortress. The restoration of the vast banqueting chamber, completed in 1860, inspired a similar undertaking in Ludwig II's castle **Neuschwanstein**. Wagner, so closely connected with the Wartburg and **Neuschwanstein** is celebrated in a museum in the Wartburgallee.

Hours of opening: summer (1 March—31 October) daily 8.30am—17.30pm; winter (1 November—28 February) daily 8.30am—17.00pm. Guided tours (45 minutes) every 5 minutes when required; at least every half hour. Telephone 03691 3001/2/3.

Denmark

*

—Copenhagen—

(Gundestrup Cauldron)

NATIONALMUSEET

Celtic cauldrons of regeneration are one of the major sources of the Grail legend. The most famous and remarkable of such vessels which can still be seen today is that discovered on the 28 May 1891 in a small peat-bog, near Gundestrup, in North Jutland. No artefact from ancient Europe, with the exception of Stonehenge, has aroused so much academic controversy and discussion. What is certain is that the cauldron, placed as an offering to the Gods, was a sacred cult object, dating from about 100 BC, venerated by whatever people—Celtic or Teutonic—were living in Denmark at the time. Depicted on it are familiar Celtic motifs, alongside others of more questionable provenance. Originally silver-gilt, it weighs 8kg and is 68cm in diameter.

Disregarding all that has been said about the Cauldron, one needs to spend some time with it and make up one's own mind as to what the images are trying to convey. Starting with the inside panel immediately to the right of the horned God Cernunnos, seated in a yoga position, we see in the lower half a procession of warriors walking towards the Great Goddess who plunges a man into a vessel (of immortality or regeneration), whilst in the top half a procession of mounted warriors rides away from her. It is not difficult to imagine that this is an initiation ceremony. The subsequent inner plates could thus be viewed as a struggle with and sacrificing of powerful inner forces until the initiate finally reaches the stage of shamanism and lordship of wild things. *(See Plate 30)*

The newly-opened Danish National Museum is the user-friendliest we know. There is plenty of time and space to view and photograph the cauldron without interference. Many other cauldrons clearly designed for religious use are also on display. What this use was is uncertain, but the likeliest explanation is that they contained the mead or wine of inspiration that played a major role in the sacred ceremonies of the Celts and Teutons.

While browsing in the museum bookshop we just happened to bump into a man whose grandfather was the minister of Gundestrup at the time of the cauldron's discovery.

The entrance to the Museum is in Ny Vestergade 10. Hours of opening: Daily 10am—5pm; Closed Mondays and on 24, 25 and 31 December. Telephone 33 13 44 11.

—Helsingor/Elsinore—

46km north of Copenhagen on the E47

Hamlet's home town is also the earthly resting place of Denmark's most famous mythical character Det Holger Dansk. Modern Danes are sensible, practical and humorous people and our enquiries for literature about him drew a blank, meeting with the amused response: 'Oh, but surely he was just an old legend?' Old legend indeed! This Danish equivalent of those once and future kings Arthur and Barbarossa was one of Charlemagne's paladins, a warrior seven feet (2.13m) tall who could drink ten pints (5.6l) without pausing for breath, almost a Gundestrup Cauldronful, and, as Ogier le Danois, performed mighty deeds through nine centuries. His lover was none other than Morgan le Fay who hauled him off to Avalon to be with her, in bliss, for at least one hundred years. She gave him a ring which restored him to youth and strength, crowned him and introduced him to King Arthur. Once, in playful mood, Morgan took the crown from his head. At that point he remembered Charlemagne and his other friends at court and longed to see them again. Morgan reluctantly let him go and he and his horse, Papillon, were conveyed by her sea-goblins from Avalon to the coast of Languedoc. He rode to Paris where he met the new king, Hugh, founder of the Capetian dynasty (cf **Senlis**), whose champion he became, raising the siege of **Chartres**. His relics were placed in the church of Belin in the Landes, south of Bordeaux, an important staging post on the road to Compostela.

His credentials as a knight of the Holy Blood are impressive. Imprisoned in Soissons during his earlier existence at the court of Charlegmagne, whose favour he had temporarily lost, he slew his captor, Bruhier, and took from him a flask containing the precious balm with which Joseph of Arimathea anointed the body of Jesus. He healed his own wounds with this and released all the knights whom Bruhier had held in his power.

His gigantic, seated, marble statue in the dungeons of Elsinore castle (conducted tours every half hour), resembling Hans Christian Andersen's description of him, still broods over past and future, awaiting the call for his return.

Austria

*

—Gurk—

Map 987, fold 39

Sinen neven er mir ze knehte liez,
Ithern, den sin herze hiez
daz aller valsch an im verswant,
den kunec von Kucumerlant.
(Your father left his nephew Ither, the king of Kukumerland,
in my charge as shield-page, in order to protect his heart
from all falseness.)

PARZIVAL 11,9,516-19

Wolfram gives us here a good example of the *langue des oiseaux,* the teasing wordplay which both hints and conceals, spilling over language boundaries. Kukumerland could be nowhere else in Europe, not even Cumberland, but Gurktal—Gurk being the German word for cucumber. So, Ither is Parzival's cousin, the Red Knight, whom he kills in his first contest, and whose armour he adopts, unaware of their relationship (cf **Alsace**). It is when Trevrizent brings home to him the gravity of this deed that he is able to feel remorse in his heart and thus be enabled to see the Grail. The Gurk/Cucumberland connection is strongly supported by the presence in Gurk of an important historical character, Saint Hemma (d. 1045), who founded the magnificent Cathedral and Abbey which completely dominates both village and valley. She married Count Wilhelm an der Sann, Sann being today that part of Slovenia which includes **Ptuj** and **Rogaska-Slatina**—the Rohitscher Berg where Trevrizent himself lived, and also the site of Wilhelm's castle. Gurk Cathedral is one of the lesser-known treasures of Austria and well worth a visit. Between Gurk and the Slovenian border on the direct road from Ptuj, you pass the extraordinary and romantic fortress of Hochosterwitz (20km south-east of Gurk) which conjures up, more than anywhere else in this part of the world, the image of the Grail Castle.

—Heiligenblut—

Map 987, fold 38

Heiligenblut (Holy Blood) derives its name from an unusual miracle. A Dane called Briccius followed his father's footsteps and, like many another Viking, enlisted in the army of the Emperor of the East in Byzantium in the early tenth century. This was a recognised career for the men of the North and for two centuries the Varangian Guard was the *corps d'élite* in Constantinople. Briccius was highly successful as a soldier and, as a good knight, rescued the Emperor's daughter from kidnappers. One day a young Jew stabbed a statue of the cruci-fied Christ to test the faith of the Christians (see Holy Blood in Introduction). To his horror blood issued from the 'wound' and the young man was later bap-tised. The Emperor, however, had the blood collected in a phial. At the same time, Briccius wished to return to his homeland. The King was sad about this and offered him in recompense for his services any wish he might request. He requested the phial of blood. Reluctantly the King consented and Briccius went on his way. Shortly afterwards, the king, regretting his generosity, sent a squad-ron of cavalry after him to retrieve the Holy Blood. Warned by divine revela-tion, Briccius took evasive action and, making an incision in his leg, hid the phial within it. The wound healed at once and Briccius, en route for Denmark, reached the approaches to the Glockner Pass just before Christmas. He was caught in a blizzard and died in a snowdrift. Three farmers, climbing up to collect the hay they had stored during the summer, saw three ears of wheat sprouting through the snow. Digging, they found the body of Briccius and, sus-pecting a miracle, brought up a pair of oxen, that had never known the yoke, to draw him whither the will of God ordained (cf **Fécamp**). The beasts halted on the site of the present pilgrimage church and refused to go any further. Before the priest from a village further down the Moll Valley could bury Briccius, the corpse raised its leg three times. The priest then discovered the phial of blood, together with a document, recounting the history of the dead man and the phial, which was deciphered by the Archbishop of Salzburg.

The present magnificent church, whose slender spire reflects the peak of the Grossglockner, Austria's highest mountain at 3797m, was built between 1430 and 1483 by the monks of Admont, founded by Saint Hemma of **Gurk**. The tabernacle is also the highest in Austria—11m—and still contains the relic of the Holy Blood and Briccius' three ears of corn. A statue shows Briccius holding the three ears of corn and pointing, like Saint Roch or Amfortas, to the wound in his leg.

Briccius was never canonised and the church is dedicated to Saint Vincent of Zaragoza who was martyred in the Grail-city of **Valencia** in 304, having been roasted on a gridiron, like his fellow deacon and martyr, the Grail-saint, Lawrence.

Briccius was presumably named after Saint Brice, the highly obstreperous successor of Saint Martin, as Bishop of Tours (see Begg, E, *The Cult of the Black Virgin*). On his feast-day the Cathars began their annual winter fast.

—Vienna—
The Hofburg Museum

Map 987, fold 40

If you are going by car make sure you have a good plan of the city and head straight for the sumptuous group of mighty, imperial buildings known as the Hofburg, where there is extensive parking. Make your way to the Schatzkammer (Imperial Treasury).

The main object of our visit to the Hofburg was the Holy Lance in Room 11, though, as we shall point out, there are many other objects of importance to be seen on the way. In sober historical terms this spearhead has been known since the eighth century and was, from the time of Kaiser Henry I, the most important item amongst the Regalia (Kleinodien). The legends surrounding it, however, lead us far afield. Its main property was as a bringer of victory: Charles Martel used it to stem the Arab invasions at the battle of Poitiers (732), and with its aid Charlemagne counterattacked, conquering Spain as far south as the Ebro. Rudolph II, King of Burgundy, was given the Lance in 921-922 by Count Samson of Northern Italy in return for driving the armies of Berengar out of his lands. Rudolph then exchanged the Lance with Henry I of Germany in return for the city of Basel and the south-west corner of the German Reich.

According to a revelation granted to J.W. Stein, Henry I sent the Spear to the English king Athelstan who, thanks to its power, annihilated the armies of the Norsemen and their allies at the battle of Brunanburh in 937. It is a historical fact that Athelstan sealed his alliance with Germany by giving his sister, Edith, in marriage to Henry's son and successor Otto I, who reigned from 936 to 973 (see **Magdeburg**). Stein adds that the Spear went with her as part of her dowry and it is certain that from this time on it has remained the palladium of the Germanic peoples. Otto carried it into battle in 955 when he crushed the invading Hungarians, who were besieging Augsburg. Frederick Barbarossa, Germany's once and future King, drowned in Cilicia bearing the Spear to the Third Crusade. In 996 Otto III had the Lance borne in front of him when he journeyed to **Rome** to be crowned Holy Roman Emperor. From then on it played a decreasing role in military history, though it was always carefully preserved from the hands of invaders such as Napoleon (see also **Karlstein**). With the other Kleinodien it spent the years from 1424-1796 in **Nürnberg**, where it was publicly displayed at Easter until 1523. In 1467 Duke Siegmund of Tirol, who had heard that wine in which the Lance had been dipped would cure stomach pains, asked for two measures to be sent from Nürnberg. During the Napoleonic wars it was preserved in Vienna, Ofen and Temesvort (Timisoara, where the Romanian freedom movement began in 1989). Its second sojourn in **Nürnberg** (1938-46) may have owed much to the faith of Hitler and his circle in its power as a talisman of victory. Ravenscroft's controversial book, *The Spear of Destiny*, deals with this matter extensively.

During the middle ages legends belonging to the spears of Saint Maurice and Longinus (see Introduction and index) became attached to the Holy Lance. These legends became further confused with traditions, dating back to Ephrem the Syrian, a fourth-century gnosticising writer, according to which a spear, belonging to Phineas, the grandson of Aaron, guardian of the Ark of the Covenant, provided a continuity in Judaeo-Christian history from Eden to Golgotha. It was thus the Spear which guarded the Tree of Life and re-admitted the fallen Adam to Eden. It was also the weapon which Saul in his madness hurled at David. Later this same lance was used by Longinus to open up the side of Christ hanging on the new Tree of Life, releasing the blood which was to fill the Grail. Finally, this sacred Spear was taken from the hands of the dying Saint Maurice, commander of the Theban legion, by the Emperor Maximian in 287 or possibly 302, at the place, now named after him in the Valais, near Martigny in Switzerland (see **Saint Maurice**).

It then became the bringer of victory to Constantine (288-337), the first Christian emperor. It was his mother, Helena, who discovered the True Cross, one nail from which is still preserved within the Spearhead. Julian the Apostate (332-363), the nephew of Constantine, sought to restore the empire to paganism and was assassinated with the Lance by Saint Mercury. These Judaeo-Christian connections might not have been altogether pleasing to Hitler, but the spear of the German Mercury, Wotan, was central to the tradition he cherished and almost certainly the major source of Teutonic spear-veneration. Wotan pierced himself with his own infallible spear, Gungnir, and hung transfixed on his tree, Yggdrasil, for nine days and nights, to bring the wisdom of the runes to human-kind. His spear never missed its mark, always brought victory and designated those heroes worthy to sit with him in Valhalla (the name given to the great temple of the Germanic soul outside **Nüremberg**).

In the same case as the Spear stands the Imperial Cross, built by Conrad II in 1024/5, to house the Spear of Destiny and a part of the True Cross. Also in Room 11 is the Reichsschwert, the sword said to be that of Saint Maurice and Charlemagne, restored around 1200, and the Reichsapfel, a crystal orb, itself a Grail according to Flavia Anderson.

Now, back to the Spear of Destiny itself. It is difficult to approach without disembodied voices warning one to stand well clear. Photography is strictly for-bidden. So, what is it one can see today? The broken spearhead, which is held together by gold, silver and copper thread and a fine gold sheath with a curi-ous inscription which covers the middle section, still emits a mysterious power, despite the security and the crowds which prevent close inspection for more than a few seconds.

Among so many fabulous objects do not miss in Room 7 the huge 2860-carat emerald, carved into a vessel in Prague in 1641. Surely, someone had in mind the medieval tradition, hinted at by Wolfram, that the Grail was an emer-ald fallen from the head of Lucifer (cf **Genoa**). In Room 8 stands a fourth-century bowl, 75cm wide, carved from a single agate in Constantinople. It was once regarded as being the Holy Grail itself, since the name of Christ could be read in the pattern of its veining. Another vessel, probably influenced by leg-ends of the Holy Grail, is the exquisite lapis lazuli bowl with an agate cameo of Leda and the Swan as its centrepiece. The child emerging from the egg must be Helen, the great quest-object of the Greeks. In Room 4 is to be seen one of the four Napkins of Veronica (cf. **Rocamadour** and **Jaén**), considered authentic.

Slovenia

*

—Ptuj—

Map 987, fold 40

We nearly missed Ptuj altogether. We had been asking tourist offices and cultural attaches in vain for some time for the whereabouts in Austria of a place called Pettau where a brook called the Greian flows into the Drau in the province of Styria.

We needed this because it was the home of Parzival's grandfather and thus fixed the Grail-Knight as a potentially historical character in time and space, and the places mentioned in his story as really existing and not merely Wolframian otherworldly inventions. We noted that the Drava flows for only a few miles through present-day Styria, so we thought that perhaps Carinthia, with which Parzival's ancestors were also connected, was the province intended. Here again we drew a blank. Then, in Wolfram's own home, **Eschenbach**, we discovered that Pettau was now the Slovenian Ptuj and that there is indeed a stream called the Grajena, which flows into the Drava at that point.

We arrived at Ptuj in late afternoon and wandered into the town centre where we discovered the brand-new tourist office in an ancient tower, still open, with a remarkably enthusiastic and helpful young man in charge. He knew nothing of Parzival or Wolfram—the Germanic connection is not highly favoured in these parts—but was horrified that we were not staying at the beautiful Hotel Mitra and did his best to persuade us to allow him to arrange a transfer.

Then we noticed on the wall of the office a magnificent map produced by G.M. Vischer in 1678, describing, in German, this part of 'the most fertile Duchy of Styria'. Suddenly we felt, across the centuries, that Parzival and his family were neighbours, as various pieces in the jigsaw began to fit together.

159

The Germans took control of this important frontier area in 874 and it soon became a judicial and customs centre, levying tolls on Drava shipping. It would have been at this time that the original castle, which housed Parzival's ancestors, dominated the town and the river. The Drava formed the boundary between the important archdioceses of Aquileia and Salzburg to which Ptuj, although south of the river, belonged. It also had close connections with the much nearer diocese of **Gurk** (q.v.). The map even showed an area called Gurkfeld on the north side of the Drava, which Saint Hemma, who lived in **Rogaska Slatina**, donated to the diocese.

Other placenames aroused our interests. Jerusalem, in the heart of a superb wine-growing district, was thus named by a group of pilgrims, setting out for the Holy Land, who came upon this earthly paradise and decided they need go no further and built a beautiful church here amid the vineyards. Not far away is Babylon. Stein relates that the race of Anjou/Anschau, the Grail family, which stems from Carinthia and Styria as well as from France, was originally a Babylonian word, Anchan. To the south-west of Ptuj and **Rogaska Slatina**, just south of the Maribor-Ljubljana motorway, lies the town of Celje. This is Zilje, which Wolfram refers to, the place whence Trevrizent, Parzival's guide and mentor, set out and encountered the hero's father, Gahmuret, *der werde Anschevin*, the true Angevin.

Ptuj castle today dates from the twelfth century with many later additions and, except for its position, bears little resemblance to Gandin, the fortress of Parzival's forebears, though one tower from the original building still stands on the western edge of the castle hill on the tournament field.

Below us, we tried to guess where the Grajena flowed into the Drava. Now it goes underground and ends ignominiously in the town waterworks before adding its contents to the dammed lake, these days used for fishing and water sports, to the south-east of the town.

Ptuj was an extremely important centre of Mithraism (three separate Mithraeums have been found here), a knightly mystery religion with many grades of initiation that was superseded by Christianity but remained an important ingredient of the spiritual Grail tradition.

—Rogaska Slatina—Rohitscher Berg—

About 30km south-west of Ptuj

Parzival's uncle, Trevrizent, tells the Grail Knight of his life and adventures. He had known love and been in its service throughout the world as far as the mountain Feimurgan (Morgan-le-Fay) and Agremontin, east of Salerno—the greatest medical school of ancient Europe founded by a Greek, a Roman, a Jew and an Arab, where women were still trained to be doctors when in all other universities such studies were forbidden. Finally, after meeting his brother-in-law, Parzival's father, Gahmuret, who gave him a precious green stone, he came to the Rohitscher Berg, where he met a party of Wends, a Slavonic-speaking people from south-east Germany and the borderlands between the Elbe and the Oder, whose name in German signifies change or turn. This encounter seems to have been a turning-point for Trevrizent for he says: 'From Rohas (Rohitscher Berg) I took my journey and unto Gandin (**Ptuj**) I came.' Here Trevrizent returned to his roots and discovered his meaning.

We went the other way round, from Gandin to Rohas, uncertain of what we sought. As we entered the mountainous region of Haloze we became increasingly aware of a mountain that we hadn't seen from **Ptuj** castle. In the pleasant spa town of Rogaska Slatina we asked at the tourist office for the most likely sacred mountain of the district. The official was in no doubt at all. It was this very mountain, Donacka gora, at 881m tiny compared with the giants around Krajnska gora, but still known as the Matterhorn of Slovenia. We knew that this was the Rohitscher Berg we saw on the old map of 1678 thai hangs in the Ptuj tourist office, and was marked as such. Its original name was Donar Berg, the sacred mountain of the Germanic god of thunder and lightning, Donar or Thor. Now he has been replaced by his near-namesake Saint Donat, an Irish missionary in the service of the Frankish kings.

Hemma of **Gurk** (d. 1045) married the local lord, Count Wilhelm of Lower Styria, who lived here, and thus became, through the Parzival connection, almost certainly a member of the Grail family. She was the foundress of the abbey which became **Gurk** cathedral.

Czech Republic

*

—Karlstein—

Map 987, fold 28

The Holy Roman Emperor, Charles IV, King of Bohemia, began to build his Grail castle, Karlstein, in 1348 on three levels, those of body, soul and spirit. His Holy of Holies, the contemplation chamber, where he meditated lovingly on the precious stones and relics that linked him to divine wisdom, is the chapel of Saint Catherine. To get to the chapel of Saint Catherine you must pass through the church of Saint Mary (Marienkirche). In the small passage that links the two there is a domed niche, about which the guides have nothing to say, known as the *Grave of Christ*. The passage from the physical world of birth, life and death to spiritual union with divine wisdom was thus represented symbolically in architecture. *(See Plate 31)*

There is a most moving painting on the walls of the Marienkirche which shows Karl in loving contemplation of a relic which most likely contained some of the Holy Blood of **Mantua**. Central to Karlstein is the church of the Holy Cross. Unfortunately, when we were there it was closed for restoration. But its centrality points to the presence of the imperial regalia brought by Karl to Karlstein (see **Trifels**) where they remained until 1424. These included the lance with which the side of Christ was pierced (see **Vienna**), a sword belonging to Saint Maurice and one which an angel gave to Charlemagne to help him defeat the heathens, as well as a crystal vessel containing precious relics. It is of interest that this vessel was a present from Peter of Lusignan, the King of Jerusalem and Cyprus and descendant of Melusine, fairy-mother of the Grail-lineage, from whom Karl was also descended. It was this vessel which he venerated as the Holy Grail from Good Friday until Easter Eve, each year in the Chapel of Saint Catherine.

162

Chrétien de Troyes describes the hall in which the knights gathered for their meals and in which they received the Grail from descending angels: 'The hall lay before the tower, and the pillared halls before it.' The Luxembourg Hall gives a very good example how this hall might have looked. It seems that at the end of the age of chivalry Karl, an avid reader of Chrétien de Troyes and Wolfram von Eschenbach and the old romances of chivalry, consciously set out to atone for the destruction of the Order of the Temple by creating, in architecture, the inner meaning of the Grail-quest.

Karl visited the relics of the Holy Blood and Longinus secretly by night in the year 1354 in **Mantua**. It is said that he left the blood intact but took back to Bohemia with him an arm and part of the shoulder of Longinus as well as, possibly, the head.

The treasures which were once preserved at Karlstein can now be seen in either the Museum of the Kingdom of Bohemia in Prague or the Hofburg of **Vienna**.

Opening hours are: 1 March to 31 March 9am-3pm; 1 April to 31 May 9am-4pm; 1 June to 31 August 8am-5pm; 1 September to 31 October 9am-4pm; 1 November to 31 December 9am-3pm; closed Mondays and the day following a feast day. Conducted tours only, in various European languages.

The road up to the castle is forbidden to cars during opening hours.

Switzerland

*

—Arlesheim—

Map 413, fold 34
Take last exit of motorway south of Basel

In 708 Saint Odile (see **Alsace, Niedermünster**) bequeathed her estate of Arlesheim to the Alsatian abbey that bears her name. Her statue, which once stood in the parish church that was dedicated to her, can now be seen in a side niche of the Dom (consecrated on 26 October 1681) above the shrine housing her relics. She is holding a Grail containing two eyes, symbolising her sight-giving properties. At the foot of the altar stands an urn of holy water to heal the eyes of the afflicted. The water is blessed on her feast day, 13 December, which she shares with that other bringer of light, Saint Lucy. The whole theme of the interior of the Dom is one of light and brilliance which is also conveyed in the magnificent painting by Guiseppe Appiani of the Annunciation (1760).

THE LEGEND OF SAINT ODILE

Saint Odile was born in the Hohenburg Castle on **Mont Saint Odile**. After many years of remaining without child, her father, Eticho, Count of Alsace, was furious when his wife gave birth to a daughter who was blind and sickly and ordered her to be killed. Her mother arranged for a nurse to hide with her in the nearby forest. Eventually, Odile was brought to a monastery where she was educated and well cared for. At her baptism she miraculously regained her sight. This miracle could not be kept a secret and Odile's parents came to hear of her whereabouts. Although Eticho did not want to see his daughter again, Odile, nevertheless, made her way back to the Hohenburg. On the way she healed a sick woman who called her 'Queen of Heaven' because of the bright light radiating from her. When Eticho killed her brother with a single blow, Odile's prayers were answered and he was restored to life. Her father's hatred eventually became unbearable for Odile and, dressed in peasant clothes, she escaped towards the south. But her father caught up with her at what is today Arlesheim. She found a grotto under the castle to hide in and, once inside, the rocks closed behind her. Eticho was hit on the brow by a falling stone and collapsed, bleeding heavily. A being of intense light appeared out of the rockface as he lay there and the Count now experienced a total conversion and was reconciled with Odile.

—Dornach—

Above **Arlesheim** and its twin village Dornach stands a modern Grail Temple, the Goetheanum, the world headquarters of Anthroposophy. Rudolf Steiner, who planned every detail of the strange asymmetrical building, was profoundly interested in the Grail as a spiritual vessel for our time. He and his followers, especially Stein, have made many valuable contributions to the history and understanding of this phenomenon. Steiner believed that near by, perhaps in the garden called the Eremitage in **Arlesheim**, Parzival and Sigune, his cousin, had their three meetings, as told by Wolfram.

—Saint Maurice—

Map 988, fold I

The Abbey of Saint Maurice was founded in 515 by King Sigismond of Burgundy who had recently converted from the Arian heresy. It attracted increasing numbers of pilgrims (not least because of its sacred spring), and was gradually extended to its present size.

Saint Maurice, hemmed in by forbidding cliffs at the narrow entry to the canton of Valais, looks a good place for a massacre—and was. Here, in the late-third century, the Theban legion, consisting of Egyptian Christian Gnostics under their commander, Maurice, refused the orders of Emperor Maximian to sacrifice to the gods of **Rome**, and carry out ethnic cleansing operations against local Celtic Christians, and were slain to a man. A sanctuary to house the relics of the martyrs was built in the second half of the fourth century by Saint

Theodore the Just of Valais. Some of these relics are kept in magnificent caskets in the *trésor* of the Basilica. The most interesting item in the treasury from our point of view is the resplendent sardonyx cup created for pagan cultic purposes in Alexandria in the first or second century BC, showing what may be the myth of Phaedra, who was enamoured of her stepson, the virgin horseman, Hippolytus. It was donated to the Abbey by Saint Martin of Tours, himself an ex-cavalryman, who filled it with a miraculous dew-fall of blood during his visit to the field where the Theban legion was martyred. On the chest of the children of Saint Sigismond, a large Saint Andrew assumes the central place normally occupied by Christ. It was he who revealed to a woman of **Mantua** the lost burial place of Longinus. His cross is the Burgundian rune for Wotan.

As well as being a miraculous blood site (there is also a spike from the crown of thorns given by Saint Louis), Saint Maurice is associated with the Spear of Destiny, which the Emperor took from the hands of the dying saint. The stone, on which Saint Maurice knelt and was decapitated, is not in the Abbey but in the chapel of Vériolez (normally open). It is 'a stone from heaven', kept on an iron grille some eight feet above the ground in a pillared shrine immediately to the right of the entrance. To find the chapel follow the road to the left, signposting the hospital, as you enter the town from the motorway exit, or from Martigny, turn left on the Avenue de Vériolez and follow signs to the chapel.

Baigent, Leigh and Lincoln are convinced that the evocatively named Sion, capital of the Valais and 30km further up the Rhone is the home-town of Parzival. If so, then why should Provence on Lake Neuchatel not be Kyot's place of origin rather than Provence or the French Provins? The Merovingians certainly took an interest in the Valais and had a mint in Sion. The Merovingian casket in the *trésor* of Saint Maurice is considered the finest in existence.

Opening hours of the *trésor* are 10.30am and 4.30pm (more frequently in summer). Ring sacristy bell for attention.

Major Texts

Arthurian Romances, de Troyes, C., trans. Owen, D. (1987).

The Death of King Arthur, trans. Cable, J. (1971).

The High History of the Holy Grail, trans. Evans, S. (undated).

Lancelot of the Lake, trans. Corley, C. (Oxford University Press 1989).

Le Morte Darthur, Malory, Sir T. (J.M. Dent & Sons Ltd. 1961).

Parzival, Wolfram von Eschenbach, Vols. I & II (Reclam 1981).

Parzival, Wolfram von Eschenbach, trans. Hatto, A.T. (Penguin 1980).

Perceval in Arthurian Romance, de Troyes, C., trans. Owen, D.D.R. (Everyman 1987).

'Peredur', in *The Mabinogion,* Guest, Lady C. (John Jones Cardiff Ltd. 1977).

Perlesvaus, The High History of the Holy Grail, trans. Evans, S. (James Clarke & Co., Cambridge, undated).

Queste del Saint Graal: La Queste du Graal, ed. Béguin, A. and Bonnefoy, Y. (Editions du Seuil 1965).

Quest of the Holy Grail: Queste del San Graal, trans. Matarasso, P.M. (Penguin 1969).

Sir Gawain and the Green Knight, trans. Stone, P. (Pengiun Classics 1959).

Select Bibliography

Alarcón, H.R., *La Otra España del Temple* (Martinez Roca 1988).

Alvarellos, L.C., *Las Leyendas Tradicionales Gallegas* (Espasa-Calpe 1977).

Anderson, F., *The Ancient Secret* (R.I.L.K.O. 1987).

Anon. *A Guide to Glastonbury's Temple of the Stars* (Watkins 1935).

Ashe, G., *Avalonian Quest* (Fontana 1984).

—*King Arthur's Avalon* (Fontana 1957).

—*The Landscape of King Arthur* (Henry Holt 1987).

Atienza, J.G., *La Rebelión del Grial* (Martinez Roca 1985).

—*Guía de la España Griálica* (Arín 1988).

Attwater, D., *Dictionary of Saints* (Penguin 1965).

Baigent, M., Leigh, R. and Lincoln, H. *The Holy Blood and the Holy Grail* (Jonathan Cape 1982).

Baigent, M., Leigh, R., *The Temple and the Lodge* (Jonathan Cape 1989).

Begg, E. and Rich, D., *On the Trail of Merlin* (Aquarian Press 1991).

Begg, E., *The Cult of the Black Virgin* (Arkana 1985).

Bertram, W. *A Royal Recluse, Ludwig II* (Martin Herpich & Son, undated).

Birks, W., and Gilbert, R.A., *The Treasure of Montségur* (Crucible 1987).

Borne, von dem G., *Der Gral in Europa* (Fisher Taschenbuch Verlag 1987).

Bouyer, L., *Les Lieux Magiques de la Légende du Graal* (O.E.I.L. Paris 1986).

Campbell, J., *Creative Mythology* (Penguin 1976).

—*The Hero with a Thousand Faces* (Paladin 1988).

Charpentier, L. *Les Mystères Templiers* (Laffont 1967).

Coincy-Saint Palais, *Le Saint Graal et le Précieux Sang* (printed by Corbière et Jugain, Alençon 1972).

Cross, F.L. (ed), *The Oxford Dictionary of the Christian Church* (London University Press, 1958).

Eschborn, M., *Karlstein* (Verlag Urachhaus 1971).

Evola, J., *Il Mistero del Graal* (Edizioni Mediterranee 1972).

Goodrich, N., *King Arthur* (Watts 1986).

Guerber, H., *Legends of the Middle Ages* (American Book Co. 1896)

Hancock, G., *The Sign and the Seal* (Heinemann 1992).

Haskins, S., *Mary Magdalen* (HarperCollins 1993).

Judith, H., *Arlesheim und Odile* (Buchdruckerei Arlesheim 1988).

Jung, C.G., *Seven Sermons to the Dead* (Stuart & Watkins 1967).

Memories, Dreams, Reflections (Collins and Routledge & Kegan Paul 1963).

Jung, E. and von Franz, M.-L., *The Grail Legend* (Hodder and Stoughton 1960).

Loomis, L., *The Grail* (Princeton University Press 1991).

Markale, J., *Brocéliande et l'Enigme du Graal* (Pygmalion 1989).

—*Le Graal* (Retz Poche 1989).

Matthews, J. and Green, M., *The Grail Seeker's Companion* (Aquarian Press 1986).

Matthews, J., *The Grail Tradition* (Element 1990).

—*At the Table of the Grail* (ed.) (Routledge & Kegan Paul 1984).

—*The Household of the Grail* (ed.) (Aquarian Press 1990).

—*The Grail Quest for the Eternal* (Thames and Hudson 1981).

Mola, S., *Castel del Monte* (Mario Adda 1992).

Nutt, A., *Studies on the Legends of the Holy Grail* (David Nutt, London 1888).

Ojeda, J., *El Santo Grial* (Nadur 1990).

Rahn, O., *Croisade Contre Le Graal,* trans. Pitrou, R. (Stock 1974).

Ravenscroft, T., *The Spear of Destiny* (Weiser 1973).

Ravenscroft, T. and Wallace-Murphy, T., *The Mark of the Beast* (Sphere Books Limited 1990).

Rolt-Wheeler, F., *Mystic Gleams from the Holy Grail* (Rider, undated).

Runciman, S., *The Medieval Manichee* (Cambridge University Press 1969).

Sinclair, A., *The Sword and the Spear* (Century 1993).

Starbird, M., *The Woman with the Alabaster Jar* (Bear and Co. 1993).

Stein, J.W., *The 9th Century, World History in the Light of the Holy Grail* (Temple Lodge Press 1988).

van der Post, Sir L., *Jung and the Story of Our Time* (Hogarth Press 1976).

von Franz, M.L., *C.G. Jung: His Myth in Our Time* (Hodder & Stoughton 1975).

Voragine, The Blessed James of, *La Leyenda Dorada* (Alianza 1982).

Walker, B., *The Women's Encyclopedia of Myths and Secrets* (Harper & Row 1983).

Wallace-Murphy, T., *Illustrated Guidebook to Rosslyn Chapel* (Friends of Rosslyn 1993).

Weston, Jessie L., *From Ritual to Romance* (Doubleday Anchor Books 1957).

Westwood, J., *Albion: A Guide to Legendary Britain* (Granada 1985).

Wood, N., *Genisis* (Baton Press 1985).

Notes on the Sources

In the bibliography we have included some of the texts that are relatively easy to find but others are unavailable in modern languages. Summaries of all the main texts can be found in *The Grail Seeker's Companion* by John Matthews and Marian Green, *The Grail* by Professor Loomis and Flavia Anderson's *The Ancient Secret*.

The text most familiar to English-speaking readers is, of course, *Le Morte Darthur*, written by Sir Thomas Malory in 1469-70, and printed by Caxton in 1485. It is a skilful selection and blending of material and inspired some of the poems in Tennyson's *The Idylls of the King*.

The first known, still existing, book about the Grail is the unfinished poem, *Le Conte del Graal* or *Perceval*, written by Chrétien de Troyes about 1180 and based in part on an earlier work given him by his patron, Philip, Count of Flanders. Four major French continuations of Chrétien's romance from different writers appeared during the following half century. The city of Troyes had very strong Templar connections as well as being a famous centre of Jewish learning. It has been plausibly argued that Chrétien's description of the Grail banquet was influenced by the Seder Passover ritual as practised by the Jews of Troyes in the twelfth century. The only notably heretical feature in Chrétien is that a woman carries the Sacrament.

SUMMARY OF CHRETIEN'S PERCEVAL

Perceval is brought up alone in a forest by his widowed mother who tries to ensure that he knows nothing of chivalry lest she lose him, like his father and brothers. Nevertheless, when he encounters three knights, whom he takes to be angels, he goes off in search of adventure, at which his mother dies of grief. He reaches Arthur's court, where he avenges the Queen by killing a knight who has insulted her and stolen the royal cup. In quest of further adventures, he arrives at the court of the Fisher King who gives him a sword. He witnesses a procession in which a squire carries a white lance from the point of which a drop of blood runs down on to his hand. Among other marvels there follows a beautiful damsel holding a Grail which emits a brilliant light. A magnificent banquet is served during which the Grail again passes before them, but Perceval, following the advice he has received from his mentor, Gornement, asks no questions about what he has seen. Next morning there is no one around and he just succeeds in crossing the drawbridge as it is being raised. Then he meets a damsel, who turns out to be his cousin, mourning her dead lover. She reveals to him that the Fisher King was wounded in the thighs and that he would have been healed if he, Perceval, had asked concerning the spear and the Grail.

Perceval returns to Arthur's court where a loathly damsel appears and scolds him for his silence, after which he vows not to lie two nights in the same lodgings until he can learn whom one served with the Grail and why the lance bled. After a lengthy interpolation describing the adventures of Gawain, Chrétien returns to Perceval who, after five years of wandering and combat, meets some pilgrims on a Good Friday. They direct Perceval, who no longer believes in God, to a hermit who reveals himself to be his uncle. He hears his confession and on Easter Day gives him Communion. Here the story of Perceval breaks off to be continued by other hands.

WOLFRAM VON ESCHENBACH

Between 1200 and 1210 a German Grail poem, *Parzival,* written by Wolfram von **Eschenbach,** appeared. This epic was considered by Joseph Campbell to be 'the first sheerly individualistic mythology of the human race'. Wolfram had read Chrétien but was informed by other sources, notably a certain troubadour, Kyot 'the Provençal', who had received the tradition from Flegetanis, a calf-worshipping astrologer of the race of Solomon in **Toledo.** One derivation of his name is FelekThani, the Arabic word for the guardian of the sphere of Mercury. Wolfram was especially interested in the Grail family and its mysterious guardians, the *Templeisen,* clearly intended to be the Templars, but Wolfram, who constantly infuses hidden meanings into his word-play, here introduces the word *Leisen,* which means the quiet ones, thus suggesting a secret branch of the Templars, those whose name and mission should not be divulged. Whereas Chrétien's interests are predominantly courtly, *Parzival* lends itself to an esoteric, even Cathar, reading and is more universal in scope. Feirefiz, Parzival's half-brother, a worshipper of Juno and Jupiter, was born in Africa, son of a Moorish queen. Wolfram is unusually sympathetic both towards Muslims and women. He admires the black Moorish queen Belacane, awards Feirefiz the Grail maiden Repanse de Schoye (Fullness of Joy) as his bride and has the Grail tended solely by women. Feirefiz's son is Prester John, the legendary priest-king of India and Ethiopia. Trevrizent, a Merlinesque teacher, Parzival's uncle, acts as his confessor without benefit of holy orders, and twelve kings of India and Ethiopia instruct Parzival that the lesson he must learn, before becoming Grail King, is compassion.

For Wolfram the Grail is a stone entrusted by angels to Titurel and his descendants. The son of Parzival is Lohengrin, the Swan Knight, whose grandson is Godefroy de Bouillon, but here we pass from myth into history. Wolfram, in some ways a highly mystical writer, is also refreshingly down to earth. His characters and places, though intentionally muddled, sound historical and geographical. This has led seekers, including ourselves, to find homes for them in various parts of Europe. To our great satisfaction, we discovered by serendipity what we are convinced is the true setting for Parzival and the Grail family in Slovenia (see **Ptuj**). It was Wolfram's work that inspired Wagner's *Parsifal*.

Robert de Boron, also writing about 1200, links the Grail specifically to the Cup of the Last Supper in which Joseph of Arimathea, described as a knight, collected the Blood of the crucified Christ. Joseph's son, Josephes, is described as the first Christian bishop and reappears four hundred years after his death to celebrate the Mass of the Grail. His uncle is Bron, the Rich Fisher. De Boron's sources include the non-canonical Gospel of Nicodemus, also known as the Acts of Pilate, and its appendix, The Avenging of the Saviour.

From the same period (c. 1200) dates the Welsh romance Peredur (Perceval). Although this seems to be based largely on Chrétien it contains much archaic Celtic material to be found nowhere else. There is no Grail as such but a head, borne on a salver, and a spear which drips blood, as well as a broken sword which the hero repairs.

Perlesvaus, translated into English as *The High History of the Holy Grail,* was written, according to Loomis, in Flanders between *c.* 1200 and *c.* 1225, though Markale detects a strong **Glastonbury** influence. Flavia Anderson argues plausibly that the missing link is none other than Saint Dunstan, Abbot of **Glastonbury**, Archbishop of Canterbury, and most important man in England until his death in 988. Suspected of black magic, he spent two years in exile at the court of Count Arnulf of Flanders. He might thus also be the author of the book given by Philip of Flanders to Chrétien. The quest in *Perlesvaus* begins when Guinevere laments to Arthur the sad decline of the Round Table. The title *Perlesvaus* (loses-his-valleys), has led some authors to see a reference to the Cathar nobles whose lands were being expropriated at this time in the Albigensian Crusade. Arthur's encounter with a woman, albeit the Virgin Mary, assisting at Mass and offering the chalice, is a further indication of unorthodox tendencies.

Didot Perceval (1190-1225) may be a prose version of a lost poem by Robert de Boron. It accords a major role to Merlin and introduces the blood of Christ borne in a vessel by a squire.

Le Grand Saint Graal or *Estoire du Saint Graal,* which Nutt dates before 1204, offers many original features amongst its complications. In 750 a hermit, while lying in his hut in the wilds of white Britain (Alba—white—is Scotland) on Maundy Thursday, is assailed by doubts concerning the Holy Trinity. Christ appears to him and gives him a book written by Himself. This consists of four parts under the following headings: 'This is the book of thy lineage; here begins the book of the Holy Grail; here is the beginning of the terrors; here begin the marvels.'

After various wonders and adventures as far afield as Norway, Christ commands him to make a copy of the book before Ascension Day. The story begins with Joseph of Arimathea, who is instructed to build an ark to contain the Grail which only he and his son Josephes may touch. They journey to Sarras, chief city of the Saracens (and also a real place in Nubia) when they visit the Temple of the Sun. They celebrate a proto-Mass before the Ark of the Grail, see red angels carrying the instruments of the Passion as well as the crucified Christ, whose blood flows into the Grail. Joseph receives the Sacraments from Christ and is consecrated Bishop. When he says Mass with the words Christ has taught him, the bread becomes a child who is divided into three parts but eaten whole. Eventually the company is transported to Britain on Joseph's shirt. Joseph is wounded in the thigh in the forest of **Brocéliande** and the parts of the sword, which broke when it struck him, will only be reunited by Galahad. Joseph dies and is buried in the Abbey of Glays in Scotland.

The Queste del Saint Graal, much of which can be found in Malory's *Le Morte Darthur,* forms part of the five-part narrative Vulgate or Lancelot-Grail Cycle, and was written between 1215 and 1235. It is the most successful attempt by orthodoxy, represented by the Cistercian Order, to incorporate the Grail legends within the bounds of Catholic faith.

Of all the Knights who set out on the quest for the Grail, Lancelot and Gawain come close, but only Galahad, Perceval and Bors fully achieve their goal within the mystical city of Sarras, and only Bors returns to tell the tale. An interesting feature is the strong emphasis given to dream-interpretation by the various holy hermits whom the Knights meet along their way. In this novel, rich in allegory, the Grail is shown as the grace of the Holy Spirit which bestows wisdom.

Sone de Nansai, probably composed in the second half of the thirteenth century in Brabant, where the last Grail Knight, Lohengrin, married the countess and vanished when she asked his name, leads its eponymous hero from Alsace to Southern Italy to Scotland and Norway. It was here that Joseph of Arimathea bore the Grail from Askalon, killed the King and married his daughter. God wounded him in the thigh and he became the Fisher King. Sone visits the island where the body of Joseph lies and sees the Grail and the Holy Spearhead at whose point hung a drop of blood. It was this story that led Goodrich to place the Grail Castle in Peel on the Isle of Man, a land both Celtic and Norse.

Diu Crone by Heinrich von dem *Türlin (c.* 1230) is one of the longest poems, with 30,041 lines. Here it is Gawain who achieves the Grail, which is a box containing bread. All the inhabitants of the glass castle are figures from another world except the magician's sister who carries the box and performs the Greek Orthodox priestly function of dividing and distributing it. A chessboard is an archaic Celtic feature, but otherwise the poem looks back on the courtly concerns of the other romances from a great distance as something that has now passed away.

Der Jüngere Titurel by Albrecht von Scharfenberg, written in the second half of the thirteenth century, concentrates on the lineage of the Grail family and the building of the Grail temple on *Munt Salwasch,* where Parzival encounters the Grail and the Grail King Amfortas, his uncle. Scharfenberg elaborates on various themes only alluded to by Wolfram, to whom for a long time this work was attributed. Titurel builds the temple in thirty years during which time the Grail, which hovers above the site, nourishes not only him and his men but also provides the precious building materials, before making it its dwelling. The finished temple is of unimaginable splendour with a revolving dome, powered by windmills, made of dark sapphire, with golden stars, and a golden sun and a silver moon.

THE UNDERGROUND STREAM

In our sketchy references to the various divergent texts, we have confined ourselves to the quirks and oddities that particularly interested us, especially those which support our contention that the Grail belongs to the underground current of alternative Christianity, that from earliest times has flowed parallel to the main stream.

What we call the underground stream of Grail-Christianity can be traced from the Gnosis of Alexandria and the Near East, through Armenia to Bulgaria and the Bogomils of Bosnia and thence through Lombardy to the Cathars of France and the Rhineland. It was in the Languedoc that it surfaced as an open rival to the Church of Rome. More local tributaries to the stream included knights, especially Templars, who had been influenced by Eastern Christian sects, and Sufism, the Gnosticism of Islam. Another influence came from the knowledge of Greece and Alexandria, translated and preserved by Arabs and Jews in the melting-pot of races which enriched each other in accessible cities such as Toledo and Gerona. Then there was Celtic Christianity or Christianised Druidism, always closer to the Near East than to Rome, which for six centuries evangelised Europe with its own tradition of monasticism, derived from the Culdees. The heresies of Visigothic Spain were not dissimilar to this.

The Cathars, Templars and the semi-independent Irish Church were suppressed by 1314, but the stream did not dry up. The Templars took refuge in Scotland and helped Bruce to win the Battle of Bannockburn. They remained there for centuries and gave birth to Scottish Freemasonry which, in turn, from the early-eighteenth century, inspired the lodges of Europe. Along with alchemy, astrology and Rosicrucianism it fed the hidden stream during the Reformation, Counter Reformation, the Age of Reason and the revolutionary era. In the past century the revival of Gnosticism, particularly Rudolf Steiner's Anthroposophy, has done much to further understanding of the Grail.

Whatever we may say of Grail-Christianity, the truth is that the myth and symbol of the receiver and transmitter of light transcends all faiths and nations. It is, for instance, no less Christian than Jewish—from its prototype, the Ark of the Covenant, through Solomon's Temple, to the heretical Jews of two millennia ago who included John the Baptist, Jesus and his followers.

One of the great Grail castles was Taq-di-Taqdis in Persia, and some have detected Zoroastrian and Mithraic strands in the Grail story. Islam has its own Grail traditions. The Alawi sect of Syria claim to have the Grail in the form of a secret version of Saint John's Gospel—like the Cathars—and in a Damascus mosque the head of John the Baptist is still venerated. But it was from India that all our Indo-European Grails—Celtic, Germanic and Greek—ultimately derived, and to India that it returned after the quest had been achieved, never to be seen again. The realm of the fabulous Prester John, to which it passed, included, as well as India, Ethiopia, where the double wisdom bloodline of Solomon and the Queen of Sheba ran in the veins of the Emperors. The Ark of the Covenant came to rest there at Axum where, as Hancock has convincingly demonstrated, the Templars, finally fulfilling the quest for which they were sent to Jerusalem, discovered it and left proof of their passing.

We have for practical reasons confined ourselves to the old Empire of the West. We visited no sites east of Bohemia and Slovenia. This meant omitting not only all the non-European Grails, but also those of Russia and of Greece where Aquarian Ganymede was cup-bearer to the gods.

Although we could not visit India, the source, where Krishna was the first Swan Knight and whose Grail drink was the soma, India, in a curious way, visited us. While on a research trip to Germany we spent a few days at Hadamar, the nearest town to Mother Meera's home in Thalheim. We attended four *darshans* in the presence of this beautiful young woman who is an avatar of the Great Mother and conveyor of Paramatman, the light behind visible light. As one gazes into her deep eyes, which each attending the ceremony is able to do, it is easy to believe that this is no metaphor. There is no sound for the two hours that the audience lasts, no more than a hundred or so people can be accommodated and no money is solicited.

A further realization that the Grail is no metaphor in India came to us, appropriately, while visiting the Chalice Well at Glastonbury. Leonard and Willa Sleath, the wardens, had just returned from Sai Baba's ashram and allowed us to taste the soma, rather like sweet glycerine, that exudes from his hands and from the hands of others, including the Sleaths, on whom he bestowed this faculty. They also gave us a little book relating how Sai Baba granted a vessel to a number of his disciples on retreat in the high Himalayas, which produced exactly the food or drink needed for them without being asked, as well as the building materials for the ashram, like Titurel's Grail.

In the days of pre-metaphorical Christianity, Joseph of Arimathea was fed by the Grail for forty years. Saint Catherine of Genoa survived for long periods of her life with no nourishment other than the Blessed Sacrament.

Now, even the Catholic Church, repository of so many wonders and mysteries, is embarrassed by anything that smacks of non-historical orthodoxy, especially the cult of saints and relics. We have tried to preserve as many of their traditions as possible, treating them as just-so stories, not concerning ourselves overmuch with historical actuality, in itself often a myth, but wondering about the meaning of the legends. What does seem clear historically is that the Grail cult in the late-twelfth century coincided with the loss of Jerusalem to Christendom. Once the Holy City was gone it had to be reinvented as a mystical goal, though Compostela and **Vézelay** might be acceptable substitutes. Much the same happened to Judaism after the fall of Jerusalem to the Romans and the end of hopes of a military solution. The Christian solution then was Christ's statement 'My Kingdom is not of this world'.

Glossary

A brief list of persons, places and things not fully explained in the text.

Amfortas, Parzival's uncle, the maimed Grail King, who was healed by Parzival asking him the Grail question: 'What ails you, uncle?'

Arthur was a Grail Knight when he led an expedition to Annwn, the underworld, to bring back the pearl-rimmed cauldron of Bran (that would not cook the food of a coward), one of the hallows of Britain. As Taliesin recounts: 'Except seven, none returned from Caer Vedwyd'.

Bagdemagus, King of Gorre (Gorron in Normandy), father of Meleagant, who kidnapped Guinevere (cf **Glastonbury**). He constructed a perilous bridge under the river Varenne at **Domfront** which no one could cross without his permission. He was killed by Gawain and his tomb can still be seen at **Saint Bomer** (the name he was known by after abandoning a life of crime for religion). Lancelot visited his tomb. In another version, Bagdemagus meets Galahad at a white abbey (**Mortain?**), takes the shield of Joseph of Arimathea which is destined for Galahad, and is severely wounded by a white knight.

Bors/Bohors is the apotheosis of the ordinary, decent man, both married and Grail knight, beset with difficult choices, who reaches Sarras and the Grail with Galahad and Perceval. He alone returns to Arthur's court to tell the tale.

Catarinella. The Grail is so obviously a symbol of the depreciated feminine principle, for loss of which the land is waste, that it seems essentially a male task to seek and retrieve it. Nevertheless, Professor Markale has discovered one late story in which it is a heroine, Catarinella, who has to undertake the quest. This perhaps prefigures the prominent role of women in the search for meaning today. They played a similar role at the outset of the Christian Age of Pisces. The story comes from Corsica where Hassan of Huesca sent the Holy Grail to Charlemagne.

The Fisher King is the head of the Grail family who dwells in the Grail Castle and guards the Grail. The first bearer of the title was Brons, brother-in-law of Joseph of Arimathea. The Fisher King in Arthur's time was Pelles.,He is often described as wounded in the genitals, lying in torment until the arrival of the knight who is to achieve the Grail and heal him with the Holy Lance. In Wolfram he is Amfortas.

Galahad is brought up by nuns and, as a youth, arrives at Arthur's court, sits in the *siege perilous*, draws the sword from the stone and achieves the Holy Grail in the company of Perceval and Bors. Tennyson has him boast: 'My strength is as the strength of ten, because my heart is pure' and through his virginity he exceeds the exploits of his father Lancelot (also called Galahad). After he achieves the Grail and becomes King of Sarras his soul is borne up to heaven by a host of angels and a hand appears to take the Grail and the spear from earthly view.

Gawain, Arthur's nephew, was probably the earliest Grail Knight as Gwalchmai, the falcon of May, the sun approaching its zenith. The cover of Anderson's *The Ancient Secret* shows Horus as a hawk-headed knight, spearing the crocodile-dragon Typhon, from a late Roman Coptic (hence possibly Gnostic) relief in the Louvre. In *Diu Crone* it is he who achieves the Grail. Elsewhere he is often derided as a womaniser in comparison to more chaste Grail heroes. He survives in Christianity in the guise of Saint George, Demetrius and other knightly saints.

Grail Lineage in Wolfram von Eschenbach and Albrecht von Scharfenberg. Parzival's first known ancestor seems to have been King Senabor of Cappadocia who had three Sons who were in Emperor Vespasian's service when Jerusalem was conquered. They all distinguished themselves and one of them, Barillus, through his marriage to the Emperor's daughter, became ruler of France. Barillus' son, Titurison, married Elysabel, the daughter of the King of Aragon. For many years they remained childless and finally made a pilgrimage to the Holy Sepulchre which resulted in Elysabel giving birth to a son, Titurel. At his birth an angel proclaimed that from a young age he would defend Christendom. Until the age of fifty he fought passionately in many wars. Then an angel brought him the message that he had been chosen for the Grail. He left his home and spent the next thirty years building the Grail Castle. When he was four hundred years old he married Richoude. Their son Frimutel, who died young, had two sons and three daughters: Amfortas, the wounded Grail King; Trevrizent, the hermit, who became Parzival's wise teacher; Schoysiane, who married Count Kyot, Duke of Catalonia, and died giving birth to her daughter Sigune; Repanse de Schoye, the Grail maiden, who married Parzival's half-brother Feirefiz, and whose son was Prester John, and Herzeloyde, Parzival's mother who was married to Gahmuret. Parzival married Condwiramurs and they had two sons, Loherangrins (Lohengrin), who grew up with his parents in the Grail Castle and Kardeiz, who was taken away to be educated by Count Kyot, to rule one day over many lands.

Klingsor (see **Ravello** and **Wartburg**), wicked magician who sought to use the magic of the Grail and Spear for his own purposes. Wolfram calls him the Duke of Terre de Labur (in fact Capua, near Naples and Lake Avernus, where Virgil descended to the underworld) and describes him as the maternal nephew of Virgil (cf **Mantua**) of Naples. When he became the lover of Iblis, Queen of Sicily, whose name is Arabic for the devil, her husband, King Ibert, had him totally castrated. Klingsor, who came from a line of famous magicians, now devoted the rest of his life to a vengeful study of black magic. Wagner placed his garden in **Ravello**. (see also **Wartburg**)

Lancelot, apparently the most French of Arthur's knights and the greatest champion of all, is almost certainly a later version of Lug of the Long Hand, the spear-bearing Celtic sun-god, by way of Lot, King of Lothian and Orkney. **Brocéliande**, **Vieux-Banvou** and Berwick Law are all claimed as his birthplace. He was raised by Nimue, the Lady of the Lake, in her underwater palace at Comper in **Brocéliande**. He left to join Arthur's Round Table and became the best knight in the world. He saw the light of the Grail and was temporarily incapacitated by it, but was unable to achieve it owing to his adulterous relationship with Arthur's queen, Guinevere. His son was Galahad, by Elaine, daughter of Pelles, the Grail King. He ended his days as a holy hermit (see **Saint-Fraimbault-de-Lassay**). Barbara Walker notes that he was a descendant of Jesus Christ in the eighth generation.

Lohengrin was the son of Parzival and the last knight to see the Grail. When he attained knighthood the Grail called him to save Elsa of Brabant from the plots of her guardian. He was drawn in a barque by a swan (probably his brother—see **Sierra de la Demanda**) to Nijmegen, or possibly Antwerp, where he rescued Elsa and became her husband. When, breaking the interdict, she asked his name, he disappeared back to the Grail Castle, leaving a sword, a horn and a ring. His grandson was Godefroy de Bouillon who liberated Jerusalem in the First Crusade in 1099.

Mélusine. Water- and snake-goddess, whose centre was Poitou. She married Raymond, Count of Poitou (see **Montserrat**) and became the ancestress of the Lusignan Kings of Jerusalem and other royal families of Europe.

Montsalvat/Montsalvatch. The mountain of salvation, the Temple of the Holy Grail that refers to **Montségur**, **Montserrat**, and **Dinas Bran** among many,

many other possible sites as far afield as **Karlstein, Castel de Monte** and Taq-di-Taqdis in Iran (see also **Grail Castles of Germany**).

Perceval/Parzival, the son of a widow who keeps him from all knowledge of knighthood, is, thanks to Chrétien, Wolfram and Wagner, the knight with whom we are most familiar. A perfect fool, he is human, all too human, and wins through by his courage, strength, perseverance and innocence. Wolfram's nickname for him, Schneid—mittendurch, is a fair translation of Trencavel, 'he who cuts well', the young Lord of Carcassonne, who lost his valleys (Perles-vaus is another of his names) to Simon de Montfort and the forces of the Albigensian Crusade. As the Welsh, historical, Peredur, he perished at the Battle of Catterick.

Siege Perilous. This is the seat at the Round Table destined for the knight who achieves the Grail and which is extremely dangerous to anyone else. It has some of the characteristics of a Celtic coronation stone (cf Lia Fail, Tara, **Ireland**).

Templars. An order of warrior-monks, officially founded in 1118, though possibly operating some years earlier, based in the remains of the Temple of Solomon in Jerusalem and charged with the secret mission of discovering the Ark of the Covenant, the Jewish prototype of the Holy Grail. This task was accomplished, according to Graham Hancock *(The Sign and the Seal,* Heinemann 1992) at Axum in Ethiopia, after the suppression of Templars in 1312 by their successors, the Order of Christ (see **Tomar**). Wolfram makes the Templars the Guardians of the Grail and its family.

Index

All Grail sites are in **bold** type.

About the Authors

Ean Begg is a Jungian analyst, writer, lecturer and broadcaster. He is the author of *Myth and Today's Consciousness* and *The Cult of the Black Virgin*. *On the Trail of Merlin* was written with his wife, Deike Begg, with whom he lives in London.

Deike Begg is an internationally known Psychosynthesis practitioner, lecturer, workshop leader, astrologer and writer. As well as the books she has written with her husband, she is also the author of *Rebirthing—Freedom from Your Past* and *Synchronicity—The Promise of Coincidence*.

978-0-595-49872-7
0-595-49872-8

Printed in the United Kingdom
by Lightning Source UK Ltd.
130991UK00001B/90/P